M000080004

ESPECIALLY FOR

....

FROM

....

DATE

....

POWER PRAYERS

DEVOTIONS
FOR MEN

GLENN HASCALL

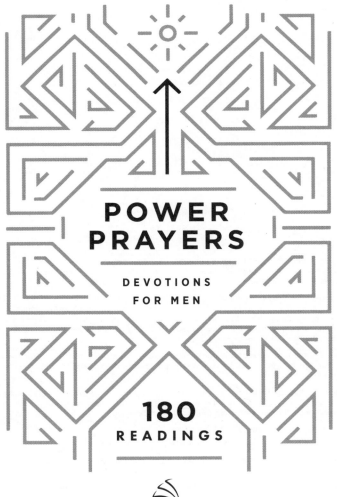

POWER PRAYERS

DEVOTIONS
FOR MEN

180
READINGS

BARBOUR
PUBLISHING

Cover Design by Greg Jackson, Thinkpen Design

Published by Barbour Publishing, Inc., 1810 Barbour Drive, Uhrichsville, Ohio 44683, www.barbourbooks.com

Our mission is to inspire the world with the life-changing message of the Bible.

Member of the
Evangelical Christian
Publishers Association

Printed in China.

GUYS, YOU KNOW THAT PRAYER IS IMPORTANT.

———————

Here is the inspiration and encouragement you need to pray regularly and with power.

According to James, prayer is a vital spiritual discipline in a righteous person's life, and this devotional will encourage you to pursue it with passion.

Throughout its 180 readings, *Power Prayers Devotions for Men* will unpack biblical examples of prayer, explaining when, where, why, and how these prayers reached God's ears and changed people's hearts.

Each entry is short and easy to read. . .but delivers a spiritual punch. Get ready for six months of inspiring, encouraging, and challenging lessons in prayer!

THE GENESIS OF HOPE

*"Be strong and courageous! Do not be
afraid or discouraged. For the LORD your
God is with you wherever you go."*
JOSHUA 1:9 NLT

Prayer is for the desperate, but it's also for lifelong followers of God.

Why did you first decide to pray? Prayer might have been your last resort during a crisis. Or maybe you prayed a memorized prayer in childhood, not really understanding whom you were praying to or why. You likely felt awkward speaking to Someone you couldn't see.

Your first prayer was ultimately a declaration of hope. You didn't want to struggle *alone*. Even if you weren't sure about God's existence, prayer was your way of proclaiming, "I hope I'm not alone."

And you weren't. You never have been. God had sought to meet you for many years, and through your first prayer, you chose to introduce yourself to Him.

First prayers are usually imperfect, but God isn't waiting for us to show off—just to show up.

*Help me take what I learn about prayer and use it to
learn how to speak to You, Father. May this learning curve
result in more meaningful conversations with You—
the God who will never abandon me.*

EXPECTING AN OUTCOME

This is the confidence we have in approaching God:
that if we ask anything according to his will, he hears us.
1 JOHN 5:14 NIV

You go to a restaurant expecting to buy food, not pet supplies. You make phone calls expecting to reach the number you've dialed. You turn your car key expecting ignition. You live with a set of expected outcomes.

When you pray, you learn to expect a listening ear, a perfect answer, and a movement in your life and circumstances. There are no outages or dropped calls in prayer. The connection is always clear and understandable.

The One who makes this promise and asks you to keep in touch is none other than the God who made you.

However, if you pray for something that the Bible forbids God's children to have, then consider the request denied. God offers forgiveness and mercy, but He never offers permission to sin. Sometimes, He says no to protect you.

God, may I never doubt that a perfect
outcome to my prayers is coming. Your answers
may not happen according to my timetable,
but help me believe You will never be late.

PRAYER CASTING

Casting all your care upon him;
for he careth for you.
1 Peter 5:7 KJV

Christians have no need for worry. If you trust God completely, you'll realize that worry is a mistake. *Always*. So when worry builds up and you don't know how to manage the crisis, just focus on the verse above.

Worry, anxiety, and fear add weight to your heart, mind, and soul. They slow you down, making you depressed and stealing your hope and joy.

The *casting* mentioned in today's verse is a reference to prayer. It's not a ritual or ceremony that eliminates worry—it's telling God that you recognize all your worry as a mistake. After you pray, you'll want to replace worry with trust, fear with faith, anxiety with belief, and cares for His comfort.

The next time you blow it, remember that prayer leads you to God's answers—even the ones you might not have been looking for.

Father, prayer is how I meet You and cast my cares.
Thanks for answering me in my insecure moments
and helping me dispose of unnecessary worry.

ATTENTION

*"[We] will give our attention to prayer
and the ministry of the word."*
ACTS 6:4 NIV

Before you begin water skiing, you must learn the basics—such as identifying pieces of equipment. However, with enough hard work and dedication, you will gradually improve. The same is true for mechanical repair, home building, parenting, and even prayer.

Giving your attention to something requires a strong interest in becoming an expert. This attention means you're teachable—and God wants to teach. Your willingness says you're devoted—and God wants you to follow. Your eagerness shows you're connected to His plan—and God wants you to understand.

All your mental resources, including prayer, come at a cost. But as God challenges your mind and heart, you will gradually learn through failed attempts how to trust and speak to Him in spirit and in truth.

Prayer requires attention that only you can give.

*God, if I ever want to know what a person
has to say, I have to pay attention. Help me
pay the same kind of attention to You.*

RAMPANT IMPERFECTION

*Don't put your servant on trial,
for no one is innocent before you.*
PSALM 143:2 NLT

Have you ever felt like your prayer life was awkward? If so, you might have been tempted to quit.

When King David tried to speak the pain in his heart, he understood that his moral shortcomings caused him to speak imperfectly to a perfect God. But he didn't give up. He kept praying the prayer of the imperfect, and God changed the king's status.

Through prayer, the guilty can stand before the Innocent, asking for and accepting God's forgiveness—despite personal failure.

Even when you are guilty, God can declare you "not guilty" when you confess your inadequacy and acknowledge His perfection. This declaration has nothing to do with your goodness and everything to do with God's gift of grace.

Your prayer life will improve when you start seeing your imperfection as the starting point of God's plan for transformation.

*Father, You never overlook sin, and I
shouldn't either. Instead of hiding, I want
to accept Your offer of forgiveness.*

NO SHOWING OFF

Hear my prayer, O LORD, give ear to my supplications:
in thy faithfulness answer me, and in thy righteousness.
PSALM 143:1 KJV

Technology has come a long way. You can transfer business calls to a cell phone, use a computer to initiate a phone call, or even join a video meeting from the cab of a tractor.

God's simple way of communication cannot be improved. If you want God's attention, pray. His faithfulness and love ensure He is standing by.

You can try to impress God, but since the One you're trying to impress made the whole universe, you'll fail every time. He asks you to seek Him in prayer, not impress Him with the talent that He gave you in the first place. Instead of impressing God, pray and let God impress you.

Showing off will never earn God's respect, but praying always gets His attention. Before you even say His name, believe He is listening. . .and then speak freely to an awesome God.

You can do what I can't, and You can walk
where I won't, Lord. Nothing is too hard for You,
and I'm amazed that You want to hear from me.

DEPRESSION

Come quickly, Lord, and answer me, for my depression deepens. Don't turn away from me, or I will die.
Psalm 143:7 nlt

Depression is a greater problem than some care to admit. It can be easy to assume that you're on your own, that no one cares or listens, and that answers are impossible to find. You can feel like a burden to others, falsely believing that everyone would be better off without you.

Some might call it a pity party, but it's real to you. Overwhelmingly real. It spreads a toxic spiritual sludge through every part of your being. When you're depressed, you will say and do things you would never normally do.

Stop. Read today's verse one more time: "Come quickly, Lord, and answer me, for my depression deepens. Don't turn away from me, or I will die."

The psalmist felt depression too, but he had an answer—seek God. Seek Him for help and for answers. Ask Him to stay with you.

Father, my prayers can express to You the pain I can't deal with on my own. The help that I need is the help that You offer.

PRAY FOR THEM

May the God of hope fill you with all joy and
peace as you trust in him, so that you may overflow
with hope by the power of the Holy Spirit.
ROMANS 15:13 NIV

Wouldn't it be fantastic to have someone pray this prayer for you? So how about praying it for someone else? Everyone needs joy, peace, and hope.

When you love others as God commanded, you should pray for them. Find a verse like the one above and use it to pray for someone else. Try saying something like, "God, You provide hope. So would You fill Bob with joy and peace as he trusts in You? That way, Bob can overflow with hope by the power of Your Spirit."

Friends pray for friends. They understand friends are important, and they want God's best for each other. So pray for your friends.

This kind of prayer is for you, but it's for others too. So make it a team effort. Others should hear what's on your heart and know that you care enough to take their concerns to God.

You have been generous enough to bring
people into my life, Lord. Help me pray for them,
encouraging them to connect with You.

TEMPTATION DENIAL

Watch and pray, that ye enter not into temptation:
the spirit indeed is willing, but the flesh is weak.
MATTHEW 26:41 KJV

Temptation is the suggestion that God's plan isn't good enough. It challenges you to step outside of God's plan just to prove to yourself that your self-discipline has been purposeless all along. Ultimately, temptation seeks to discredit God by convincing you to disregard His will and walk away.

For those who are tempted, God offers a two-pronged approach: (1) *Watch*. Carefully choose what you allow to influence your journey. Wrong messengers always bring wrong messages. (2) *Pray*. God isn't surprised by temptation; rather, He rejoices in your decision to remain on the path He's chosen for you. So keep your line of communication with Him open.

If you've ever had an addiction, you know how hard it is to keep from satisfying your body's cravings. But the urges will weaken whenever God's Spirit reminds you of His better plan.

Temptation can be confusing and frustrating
for me, God. The battle never stops.
My victory will only come if I watch and pray,
relying on You to help me stay on track.

OVERWHELMED

I am losing all hope; I am paralyzed with fear.
PSALM 143:4 NLT

You feel stretched thin. If your life were a piece of elastic, it would be ready to snap. If one more thing gets added to your plate, you might just drop the plate altogether. You're not strong enough, and that's the point.

Prayer is for the overwhelmed. It's okay when you make desperate pleas from a frantic and fractured heart. Stress and nagging anxiety are big issues that plague everyone, so when you utter words like ones in the verse above, it's not the first time God has heard them. Don't lose hope. Don't be crippled by fear. Tell God about your problems, and let Him lead you through this unwelcoming valley into a place where trust replaces fear and hope regains its power.

You can't see what God sees, and you are clueless about the things He knows. So when He walks you through the unknown, you have to trust Him, believing He has a greater purpose.

*Father, thank You for walking confidently
before me and compassionately behind me,
yet somehow never leaving my side. When
I'm overwhelmed, remind me of Your truth.*

PRAYED FOR

"I will remain in the world no longer, but they are still in the world, and I am coming to you. Holy Father, protect them by the power of your name, the name you gave me, so that they may be one as we are one."
JOHN 17:11 NIV

Jesus prayed for you. Knowing that trouble would come to His family, Jesus wanted God, His Father, to protect you.

This prayer came near the end of Jesus' time on earth. He would soon return to His Father, but His family would still need to walk in a troubled world—and Jesus did not want you to walk alone.

Jesus had seen the worst of humanity, but He also saw how much His compassion changed people. However, after He left, would His finished work on the cross be remembered? Would His friends still stand together in sharing the message of God's great rescue?

He knew, of course, that they could with God's help—and that's exactly why He prayed.

Lord, I'm so glad Jesus prayed for me and everyone who would follow You. Thanks for walking with me and protecting me on my journey with You.

UNIFIED

Neither pray I for these alone, but for them also
which shall believe on me through their word;
That they all may be one; as thou, Father, art in
me, and I in thee, that they also may be one in us:
that the world may believe that thou hast sent me.
JOHN 17:20–21 KJV

Jesus prayed for His disciples and for everyone who would ever hear His followers' message and accept His rescue.

Today's passage and yesterday's have a common theme: *unity*. One of the primary points of these verses is that Jesus and the Father are united in thought and action. God expects a man like you to follow this example, uniting your words and actions with His. But there's an additional step: finding a place of unity with other followers of Jesus. Don't disqualify someone from being a brother or sister in Jesus Christ because of personal differences.

Unity is a key theme in Jesus' prayer, and it makes perfect sense for us to pray for it today.

Getting along with other Christians is something You
don't want me to see as optional. When I follow You,
God, help me walk with others who are doing the same.

THE IMPORTANCE OF OTHERS

*God knows how often I pray for you. Day and night I bring
you and your needs in prayer to God, whom I serve with
all my heart by spreading the Good News about his Son.*
ROMANS 1:9 NLT

Other people are important to you, right? If they needed
something, you would help. Their opinions matter to you.
Their success brings a smile to your face. Their setbacks
concern you.

These people can be friends, coworkers, neighbors,
and family members. Whenever you let them into your
life, they become important enough for you to want the
best for them.

The apostle Paul had those types of friends in Rome.
He took what he was learning about prayer and applied it
to his God-given relationships. Everyone benefits from this
selfless kind of prayer.

Instead of praying only about his problems (although
this should be a part of prayer), Paul considered it an honor
to pray for those who needed God's encouragement. You
can too.

*Help me remember that people are important
to You, Father. May they be important enough
to me that I count it an honor to pray for
them, wanting Your best for their journey.*

NO HELP NEEDED

Teach me to do your will, for you are my God;
may your good Spirit lead me on level ground.
PSALM 143:10 NIV

If you believe you know everything, prayer makes no sense. Why pray for help when you can help yourself? Why ask questions when you already have the answers? Why ask God to help others when you believe they can find the answers through common sense?

Decent people make good decisions. They do their level best to find solutions to difficult problems, and they might even believe they are saving God trouble by helping others. Because these people believe they do not need God's help, they are less likely to pray.

Submission is a foreign concept to those who think they can save themselves. But if you feel this way, you can't be taught by God. You'll never feel the need to be led as long as you believe you know where you're going.

If you find yourself in this place, now is the perfect time to pray.

Sometimes, I'm arrogant enough to believe I don't
really need Your help, Lord. May I learn to realize
You've always known more than I ever will.

THE BLESSING

*The L*ord *bless thee, and keep thee: The L*ord *make his face shine upon thee, and be gracious unto thee: The L*ord *lift up his countenance upon thee, and give thee peace.*
Numbers 6:24–26 kjv

When you were a kid, you probably didn't like it when your parents or grandparents gave a sibling or another child too much attention. If you had had your way, they would've paid all their attention to you.

Today's verse is a prayer for grown-ups. It recognizes the value of sharing, the importance of selflessness, and the thrill of championing someone else's future.

This prayer desires for another person what most people want only for themselves. Aaron, the priest, asked God to bless, protect, and show His favor to someone else. He wanted peace for another person. That is why we call this kind of prayer a blessing.

A blessing can change someone's future. Everyone—including you—feels insecure sometimes, but hope arrives when people know you're praying for them. They can feel the blessing.

God, even when I don't have the motivation to pray for others, remind me of the encouragement I receive when I know others are praying for me.

TOGETHER

Confess your sins to each other and pray for each other so that you may be healed. The earnest prayer of a righteous person has great power and produces wonderful results.

JAMES 5:16 NLT

Healing is possible for those who understand, care for, and pray about each other's needs. Whenever those who believe in God's saving power have positive and unified relationships, a fellowship of the forgiven is born.

The significance of transparency and authenticity between Christians cannot be understated. It's important. Vitally important. James describes this connection as a healing force—maybe because when you share your struggles, others learn how to pray and find encouragement, knowing they are not alone in their personal tribulations.

Praying with others invites them to engage with your trials. . .and you with theirs. The logical outcome is more support, encouragement, and hope.

If the prayer of one righteous person is powerful, imagine what the prayer of many can do!

When I pray by myself, You share in my personal struggles, Father. When I pray with Christian friends, I am encouraged to keep praying. Lead me to those kinds of friends.

LIFE ENTRUSTED

Let the morning bring me word of your unfailing love,
for I have put my trust in you. Show me the way
I should go, for to you I entrust my life.
PSALM 143:8 NIV

God's people should believe that every new morning brings new opportunities. Rise to greet the day with joy in your heart and praise on your lips. Ignore the potential downsides to a story. Seek the kernel of redemption in everything you hear, remember, and share.

You can go to bed tonight with the weight of the world on your chest, or you can close your eyes knowing that God's unfailing love will greet you at dawn.

There is a direction you should follow, and God has the map. You've given your life to the God who loves and leads, so the weight of the world is not yours to carry. God can and will carry that weight, and for Him it's no hardship.

Do you trust Him?

When I'm directionless, Lord, help me remember You're not.
Wherever You lead, give me the courage to follow. When
I sleep, help me remember I can trust You with my life.

HIS COURAGE

Be careful for nothing; but in every thing by prayer and supplication with thanksgiving let your requests be made known unto God.
PHILIPPIANS 4:6 KJV

You probably can't share a personal story of how worrying gave you strength and courage. Why? Because all these positive attributes result from trust, not from disbelief.

Even at its weakest, prayer reflects the desire to believe, the need for strength, and the hope that you can be brave. At its best, prayer is the strong and courageous man's most potent tool. You don't have to be brave to pray, but praying does make you brave. You may not feel strong when you call on God's name, but His answers will give you strength. Even if you lack courage in your own abilities, His courage is enough for both of you.

So take your darkest fears and tell God all about them. Ask Him for help, seek His guidance, and express your gratitude. There's fresh power in the prayers of the weak.

God, I don't want to be so fearful of my surroundings that I'm afraid of You too. May Your strength hold me above my fear, where I can feel and learn from Your courage.

FROM DEATH ROW

*Jesus said, "Father, forgive them, for they
don't know what they are doing."*
LUKE 23:34 NLT

As His human body died on the cross, Jesus prayed for those who failed to follow God. He didn't pray for revenge—He prayed for mercy.

God would've been justified in destroying those who tried to thwart His plan, but He was also strong enough to rescue them.

Jesus recognized that God's knowledge was higher than humanity's. He knew that the people who called for His death had no idea they were killing God's Son.

You can apply this prayer to yourself too. It's possible to believe your decisions are right when they are actually opposed to God's overarching plan. But by making a regular investment in God's Word, your vision will become more closely aligned with His.

Always remember this: Jesus' plea from His place on death row means the Son of God would rather see you forgiven than condemned.

*Father, forgive me, for I don't know what I'm doing.
I am grateful You would rather show grace than
seek revenge for my lack of understanding.*

THE GREAT BUY-BACK

---

*In [Jesus] we have redemption through his
blood, the forgiveness of sins, in accordance
with the riches of God's grace.*
EPHESIANS 1:7 NIV

When Jesus asked God to forgive sinners for their lack of
understanding, He was in the process of sacrificing His
own life to redeem—or buy back—the lives of those who
were sold out to sin.

Jesus wants you to be forgiven. He gave everything He
had so that you could come to God, confess your sin (tell
Him that He was right and you were wrong), and accept
God's forgiveness.

God, in His wisdom and grace, accepted Jesus' sacrifice, thus changing the way humanity interacts with God.
There's no more separation. Access is possible. Purpose
can be identified.

Even when you feel worthless, as if your best moments
were in the past, God wants to redeem the broken pieces
of your life. He loves you more than anyone else ever has.

*Thank You for Your gift of love, Lord. No
one else could ever do that for me, so I
don't want to forget it or make it cheap.*

CONNECT OR RECONNECT

*Blessed be God, which hath not turned
away my prayer, nor his mercy from me.*
PSALM 66:20 KJV

Whether it's a friend or family member, you probably have someone you no longer speak with. You may remember what caused the falling out, or maybe the reason has been lost to time. Either way, you (or the other person) have made the choice never to speak again.

God, however, never chooses to stop talking or listening. He keeps a line of communication open to you. Sin—something which God is incapable of—is the only thing that can break the connection, disrupting the conversation until you admit that God's commands are right and that your actions have been wrong.

Admitting your sin to God invites Him back into the conversation, and He responds with forgiveness, compassion, and mercy. There may be consequences for your past choices, but you'll never benefit from keeping God at arm's length.

*May my prayers be full disclosures, God. I
don't want to hide from You things that You
already know. Help me release my stubbornness
and agree with You when I'm wrong.*

SURRENDER AND WIN

*The LORD is close to all who call on him,
yes, to all who call on him in truth.*
PSALM 145:18 NLT

Many times, surrender is less about admitting you've lost and more about admitting you've left a futile life in favor of a purposeful one. However, pride tries to prevent you from seeing that God's plan leads to a better outcome.

When you stood opposed to God, demanding your own way, was there any reason to believe He would offer you mercy? You probably couldn't imagine that He would give you a new purpose, passion, and plan.

By surrendering, you will discover freedom instead of a prison cell. Give up your plan, and the God to whom you've surrendered will empower you.

Surrender and win big, trading all your worthless things for a gift of incalculable value. The winning team receives armor, mercy, and gifts, and God stays close to those who answer to Him. Surrendering who you are for what God can make you has unimaginable benefits.

Help me choose the winning side by surrendering to You, Father. Let me resist the temptation to return to what I've left behind. Stay close to this new creation.

LEARNING AN ALTERED REQUEST

*Dear friends, if our hearts do not condemn us,
we have confidence before God and receive
from him anything we ask, because we keep
his commands and do what pleases him.*
1 JOHN 3:21–22 NIV

If breaking God's law results in a disconnect between you and God, then obedience opens unexpected doors. Sin can slow your spiritual growth, but forgiveness lets you change direction.

If your children break the rules, you must help them learn from their mistakes before they can change course. Without discipline, they'll never move forward.

God has many blessings available for you, some of which you may not be ready for yet. He can't say yes to every request, because those requests could keep you from growing the way you need.

The Bible says we can receive anything we ask from God, provided that "our hearts do not condemn us" and that we "keep His commandments and do what pleases Him."

*Help me learn more about Your plan, Lord, so
that I can pray for the things that You want
to happen. Perhaps I'll then discover requests
that You've been waiting for me to make.*

PAIN AND UNFAIR TREATMENT

For the enemy hath persecuted my soul; he hath smitten my life down to the ground; he hath made me to dwell in darkness, as those that have been long dead.
PSALM 143:3 KJV

You've probably received an unwanted delivery of pain at one point—be it physical, emotional, or mental. You weren't expecting it, but this delivery didn't have a return policy.

You could attempt to keep the box closed, but you will face what's inside eventually. Giving it away only brings pain to others while never reducing your own. You might try hiding it, but it will never leave.

King David, Israel's greatest king, faced a similar struggle. As his crisis of pain and unfair treatment reached its lowest point, he was undoubtedly tempted to wallow in his misery—but instead, he prayed. Reaching for the right words, David described to God what he faced. He sought comfort for his heart, revival for his spirit, and restoration for his soul.

God, King David is a good example of a struggler who prayed. Help me use my words to seek Your help when I'm in pain. Help me refuse to pass the pain on to others.

A SPIRITUAL 214

"I brought glory to you here on earth by completing the work you gave me to do."
JOHN 17:4 NLT

Many first responders fill out a form called a 214. It acts as a journal, describing what they did during an emergency and when. The form is useful for recalling the day's events because it's easy to forget details during a crisis.

Prayer can be your 214 report to God. Use it to share your progress, setbacks, challenges, and successes. Use prayer as a real-time chronicle of what you've faced and how you came through it. Write things down so that you can refer to your progress later.

Use prayer as an information depository, telling God how you feel, what you're facing, and the help you need. You can tell your stories of answered prayers to family, friends, and future generations. Your prayer can serve as a lamp post of God's faithfulness, and your remembrance can allow others to see His footprints in your life.

Your faithfulness shows up in my progress reports, Father. When my struggle meets Your grace, I remember that You give me what I never deserve. Help me share my story.

BURDEN LIFTER

*"Come to me, all you who are weary
and burdened, and I will give you rest."*
MATTHEW 11:28 NIV

Prayer isn't just an option—it's an invitation. It's a request to join the world's only eternal change agent. You have a body that will get sick, need sleep, and eventually die. You wear out, but God never does.

When Jesus said, "Come to me," He was talking to the overworked, overwhelmed, and overtaken. Does that sound like you?

When you come to Him in prayer, He links your limitations with His unlimited resources. After you recognize what you can't do, you will be impressed to see what God can do. If you don't come to Him, you will never be introduced to the antidote for weariness and burden. Any imitation always falls short. Relax, put soothing colors on your walls, and use pleasing fragrances all you want, but these techniques will never rescue you from worry and sin.

Only One can do that—and He already has.

*Being weary makes me want to give up, Lord.
My burdens are forcing me into impossible
tasks that I know I'll fail. Give me the rest
You promised and the hope I need.*

BACK IN A FEW MINUTES?

At midnight I will rise to give thanks unto thee because of thy righteous judgments.
PSALM 119:62 KJV

Small shops often have clock-shaped signs in their windows that read "Back in a few minutes." Such notes can be annoying: if you've made a special trip there and you're on a schedule, you may just skip the visit.

You probably understand that one person might be running the shop. That person will need to eat lunch or take a deposit to the bank. The owner has no alternative or backup—just a reliance on the customers' good graces.

Can you imagine praying, only to discover that God is taking a break? Thankfully, however, there is no bad time to pray. God's never out for an appointment or a sick day, and He never says, "Do not disturb."

If you're troubled in the middle of the night, call on the name of your listening Father. You're never a burden, and you never annoy Him.

God, I'm thankful that You never treat my prayers like irritating distractions. When I am stressed, let me pour every fiber of my being into a connected conversation with You.

SOMETHING YOU CAN DO

I can never escape from your Spirit! I can never get
away from your presence! If I go up to heaven,
you are there; if I go down to the grave, you are
there. If I ride the wings of the morning, if I dwell
by the farthest oceans, even there your hand will
guide me, and your strength will support me.
PSALM 139:7–10 NLT

Why would anyone run away from God? It's not helpful—
God is everywhere. It's like a divine game of hide and seek,
except you can't hide and He is always seeking. You can't
get away from God. Even though He knows you will try, He
prefers that you do not.

Whether in life or death, heaven or earth, on land or
on the high seas, God can meet you there. Guidance and
strength are in His presence.

Pray to God knowing that He goes wherever you go,
and then invite His presence into your life. By doing this,
you are recognizing that He's with you and that you want
to be close to Him. Even when you cannot do anything
else, you can always pray.

There's no fear when I choose Your love, Father.
You always walk with me, but it means more when
I recognize Your closeness. Let's walk together.

THE PRAYER GATEWAY

Pray in the Spirit on all occasions with all kinds of prayers and requests. With this in mind, be alert and always keep on praying for all the Lord's people.
EPHESIANS 6:18 NIV

Acknowledging God's presence, accepting His rescue, and inviting His Spirit into your life—these are the gateway to prayer. When you pray, fix your mind on God, allowing His Spirit to help you say the right words. Sometimes, you'll have no idea what to pray, but that's exactly when His Spirit helps.

God welcomes a beginner's prayer. You don't need a degree to talk with God; rather, His Spirit will gradually teach you to become more comfortable, making your conversations with Him hopeful and welcoming. It might take a little time, but you will gradually grow closer to the God who forever protects and loves you.

So use that connection with God's Spirit to learn, grow, and pray. Change is coming.

Lord, You sent Your Spirit to teach me because You know what I need. Help me use His teachings to pray in a way that pleases You and satisfies my soul.

BECOME ENROLLED

The Holy Spirit helps us in our weakness.
For example, we don't know what God wants
us to pray for. But the Holy Spirit prays for us with
groanings that cannot be expressed in words.
ROMANS 8:26 NLT

If you want to pray the powerful prayers of the righteous, you will need help when you're weak.

God's Spirit can help. You can learn what to pray for and how, but when powerful emotions overwhelm you, you'll need the Holy Spirit to pray for you. And the Bible says He does. Wouldn't you want God's Spirit to say just the right thing to God—on your behalf?

You may never know when that happens, but it's comforting to know that God has a plan whenever you can't seem to find the words.

It's possible that you've never given much thought to God's Spirit, but He came to give you guidance, teach you, and bring you God's comfort. Enroll in His classes and discover wisdom.

God, thanks for offering so many gifts for my good
and for Your glory. Thanks for the gift of Your
Spirit and for His willingness to pray for me.

HE GAVE A MASTER CLASS

It came to pass, that, as [Jesus] was praying in a certain place, when he ceased, one of his disciples said unto him, Lord, teach us to pray.
LUKE 11:1 KJV

Directly after hearing Jesus pray, one of His disciples asked Him to conduct a master class on prayer. In essence, he was saying, "We've heard You pray, but how do *we* do it?" It's not as if the disciples had never prayed or heard others pray. In fact, plenty of people in those days made proud displays of their own prayers. But this disciple was impressed by Jesus' prayer. It was authentic and intimate, and it portrayed God as approachable. How could someone pray like that?

God's Spirit can teach you how to pray, and so can Jesus' answer to His disciples' question. Scripture records this answer for your benefit, so for the next few days, sit with the disciples at Jesus' feet and learn the value of the Lord's Prayer.

Every day, I'm learning more about You and the value of praying to You, Father. I'm a guest in Your presence, but You accept me as a family member. I stand amazed.

FATHER

[Jesus] said to them, "When you pray, say:
'Father, hallowed be your name.'"
LUKE 11:2 NIV

Jesus, the Son of God, taught this lesson to all His disciples.

He didn't say, "If you pray." He said, "when"—implying that His audience was already accustomed to praying. Jesus' lesson was meant to enhance their prayer lives.

Look at the first word of this prayer: Father. This is an intimate name—one that a son would use when encountering God. Jesus' prayer seems to indicate that this close relationship should be yours as well. You are His child. He is your Father.

"Hallowed be your name." The word hallowed simply means holy, sacred, anointed, divine, and honored. The one who prays should treat God with the respect He deserves. God is your friend and He loves to spend time with you, but He's not just a buddy. His name is holy, and everything you will ever need comes from His holy storehouse.

Lord, help me to pray. And when I do, may I
honor You and recognize that You're holy.

THE ONE WHO REIGNS

Thy kingdom come. Thy will be done,
as in heaven, so in earth.
LUKE 11:2 KJV

"Thy kingdom come." Jesus knew what God's kingdom would be like. Having lived more than thirty years on earth, He had seen the world's various kingdoms, and He knew none of them could solve mankind's problems. Jesus saw justice being denied for some people. He saw sinners leading sinners, but He knew something better was coming—a kingdom that God Himself would rule—and He encouraged you to pray for this kingdom.

Jesus prayed that God would use His power to perform His will until that time arrived. He wanted God to actualize His objectives everywhere—not just in heaven, where sin cannot corrupt, but on earth, where evil runs unfettered.

God's kingdom is a reality that's so much better than your daily experiences, and Jesus encourages you to ask for it to come. This declaration begins as a prayer, but it soon evolves into a heartfelt cry that is evidenced by your personal choices.

God, Your kingdom will be worth the wait,
but I'm longing for Your future to come today.
Keep me in this state of constant anticipation.

FOOD FOR ALL

"Give us each day the food we need."
LUKE 11:3 NLT

One verse. Eight words. Less than five seconds to read. Yet this sentence is more than a mealtime blessing.

Give: this word is a request to God that acknowledges His ability to provide.

Us: suddenly, this prayer becomes a prayer of inclusion. Taking others into consideration, it selflessly asks God to go big in His provision. It invites you to name names as you ask for God's help in the lives of others.

Each day: this will not be a one-time prayer. You will come back tomorrow and spend more time with your Father.

The food: this could mean every kind of food—physical, spiritual, and intellectual.

We need: food is a blessed provision that's as necessary as air or water.

So much blessing in these eight words! Jesus' model prayer includes others, makes prayer daily, and emphasizes God's ability to provide for more than your personal needs.

Father, may I seek Your blessings for all and give
You credit for the help You provide every day.

FORGIVENESS. OFFER IT.

*And forgive us our sins; for we also forgive
every one that is indebted to us.*
LUKE 11:4 KJV

This part of Jesus' model prayer dismisses an argument that you might have made against praying for others. Perhaps you believe that you can be a good person and pray only for your friends and family. It just feels right and honest to pray for them, and they should feel grateful that you took the time to do so. However, just as the word *us* in the previous verse means you should pray for everyone, its presence here implies that you need to forgive *all* people. That way, nothing will prevent you from praying for them.

You need God's forgiveness, so ask for it. People need your forgiveness, so offer it. Love doesn't keep track of offenses, and it is quick to forgive.

If prayer includes everyone, then asking God for a clean slate means offering a clean slate to others. The Lord's Prayer is a group effort.

*Lord, Your followers have not always been authentic.
Forgive us, and may we forgive those who have hurt
us so that we can share Your love freely with all.*

TEMPTED

And lead us not into temptation; but deliver us from evil.
LUKE 11:4 KJV

God isn't in the business of temptation (see James 1:13). It would be absurd to think that He would define the rules of the Christian life and then try His best to convince you to disobey them. So why does Jesus say we should ask God, "Lead us not into temptation"?

Bible scholars have suggested two ideas: we should ask God (1) to keep us from giving in to temptation or (2) that He would keep us from being tested. Perhaps the key point is that since temptation comes to all people, you should pray for protection before you're tempted rather than waiting until temptation arrives to ask for help (although you should do the latter as well).

Jesus knew that one who is protected in battle will not be wounded as severely as the one who is unprepared when Satan attacks.

Turn my feet away from walking toward evil, God. Protect me and deliver me. May I be quick to follow Your directions so that I can experience abundant life.

KINGDOM. POWER. GLORY. FOREVER.

For thine is the kingdom, and the power, and the glory, for ever.
MATTHEW 6:13 KJV

The Lord's Prayer ends the same way it begins. Jesus—after praying that His Father's kingdom would arrive, emphasizing personal relationships and faith in God's provision, and telling His followers to treat God with respect—finished by highlighting three components to God's eternal plan:

1. *Kingdom*: this is an undefiled place where evil never exists, where needs are perpetually met, and where all things are new.
2. *Power*: the God who protects you on earth is the same God who will bring His kingdom to reality.
3. *Glory*: God doesn't need to subcontract His work because He's too overwhelmed or tired to complete it on His own. His glory is not transferrable.

Jesus knows how important it is for you to recognize God's unimaginable splendor. His ways of thinking are different. His plans are big. His future is perfect.

End your conversations with God by remembering His power to answer prayer.

It's easy to become so familiar with Your Son's model prayer that I miss the point, Father. You care for me and Your power protects me. Thank You for being strong enough to provide all my needs.

COMPANIONS

---

*All praise to God, the Father of our Lord Jesus Christ,
who has blessed us with every spiritual blessing in the
heavenly realms because we are united with Christ.*
EPHESIANS 1:3 NLT

We don't know exactly what circumstances led the apostle Paul to write these words, but it's not hard to imagine that he saw spiritual growth in those who accepted God's great rescue. These people worked together, lived together, and loved others together.

Paul understood that God's blessings lay in the center of their unity, so he praised God for approving of their actions. Paul described this unity as the body of Jesus Christ, in which each person serves a specific purpose that helps accomplish God's plan on earth (see 1 Corinthians 12:12–27).

Working with others for the sake of spreading God's message and plan is incredibly effective. The obedience involved in such a cooperation pleases Him and demonstrates that you trust His ability to help His followers.

How does your prayer life demonstrate your willingness to work with God's people?

*Every follower is important to You, Lord. Help
me work with them all to serve You even better.
Thanks for blessing me with companionship.*

A TOGETHER WORK

Just as a body, though one, has many parts, but all its many parts form one body, so it is with Christ.
1 CORINTHIANS 12:12 NIV

There are many kinds of medical tests, but all are designed to pinpoint issues that hinder the human body's effectiveness. These include eye exams, blood screens, and heart tests. People take these tests to learn what treatments will keep their body parts working together.

God has one test that determines the effectiveness of Christians: whether or not they love each other.

Without love, Christians will dispute over who is more important. They will want to be something God didn't design them to be, failing to realize the value of their place in the body of Jesus Christ.

God has graciously set you within a body of believers that works together to serve His purpose on earth, and prayer keeps all of you linked to Him.

God, help me to want what You want for me and to be happy for those who do something different— even if I think their work is more or less important.

CALLING FAITHFUL SERVANTS

Well done, good and faithful servant; thou hast been faithful over a few things, I will make thee ruler over many things: enter thou into the joy of thy lord.
MATTHEW 25:23 KJV

Jesus told a story of three men who held equal responsibility. Their master had varying degrees of trust in his managers, so while he was out of town, he assigned them the same task with different amounts of resources. Two men ended up with twice the amount they started with, but the third sat on the sidelines, protecting the resources he had and doing nothing to gain more.

When the boss returned, he labeled the first two as faithful and told them, "Well done."

Apply this to your prayer life. You could protect what you've learned and try not to upset God, or you could ask Him to help you do something with what you've been given.

You have access to God, and He's waiting to hear from you and help. God wants to see what you do with His assistance and say, "Well done."

The three managers in the story couldn't ask their boss for help, but I can ask You, God. May You hear from me often. Perhaps You will look at what I and other believers have done and say, "Well done."

THE WORK OF PRAYER

Work willingly at whatever you do, as though you were working for the Lord rather than for people. Remember that the Lord will give you an inheritance as your reward, and that the Master you are serving is Christ.
Colossians 3:23–24 nlt

What's your work ethic when it comes to prayer? Maybe you started on an "as needed" basis, but now you've determined you don't need God's help as much, so you only pray when something big happens.

However, if prayer isn't a skill, then neither is language—which would mean we'd all be speaking in gibberish. Apply strong effort to your prayers, continuously learning how to have transparent and authentic dialogues with God.

Think of it this way: the conversations you had with your dad or grandpa when you were five weren't the same ones you had after you graduated. The more you learn about the other person, the more your interests in that person will grow.

How might this apply to your prayer life?

Lord, having conversations with You can seem a bit like work until I learn to be comfortable. Help me trust You with my concerns as I learn to pray.

HE SHOWS UP

I spread out my hands to you;
I thirst for you like a parched land.
PSALM 143:6 NIV

Praying to God can feel like watching the skies for rain, gazing at a field of wheat and needing fresh bread, or witnessing love in action while craving to be loved.

When King David reached out to God, he burned for a connection that would meet his needs. David didn't have a "tall glass of water" need—he had an "entire landscape that hadn't felt a raindrop in ages" need. He had a withering, wilting sense of impending death. David prayed, knowing that if God delivered the clouds to send the rain, everything would be okay. If not, he would be faced with a devastating loss.

You may be tested at certain times in your life, but these trials are meant to alert you to a need while also reminding you of God's ability to provide. When God finally shows up, you'll witness His miraculous answer to your prayer.

Thanks for showing up when I'm unable to control my circumstances, God. Help me recognize Your miracles and honor You.

GOD CAN'T BE FOOLED

If I say, Surely the darkness shall cover me; even the night shall be light about me. Yea, the darkness hideth not from thee; but the night shineth as the day: the darkness and the light are both alike to thee.
PSALM 139:11–12 KJV

The Bible clearly teaches that the way you do things and the way God does things cannot be compared (see Isaiah 55:8). Total darkness surrounds you, preventing you from seeing anything. But darkness hides nothing from God. When people think they can keep secrets from God, they don't understand that nothing can be hidden from Him. Nothing is a surprise to God.

This fact shouldn't feel like an invasion of privacy; rather, it should be an encouragement. Nothing that happens to you will ever catch God off guard. To Him, there is no difference between light and dark.

Feel free to tell God even your darkest fears and secrets, knowing that He cannot be fooled or surprised.

My life and the plans I make are an open book to You, Father. Help me appreciate the fact that nothing takes You by surprise.

EASE FEAR'S FIRM GRIP

It is impossible to please God without faith. Anyone who wants to come to him must believe that God exists and that he rewards those who sincerely seek him.
HEBREWS 11:6 NLT

Do you find it easy to talk about your problems to people you don't trust? Do you tell them about your dreams for the future? No? Why not?

You probably keep information from those you don't trust, and you may even avoid any interactions. A lack of trust invites fear, and fear makes love foreign and unattainable.

Faith, on the other hand, is the only thing that can please God. You can either trust Him or be afraid of Him—it's impossible to do both. He exists. (Believe it.) He blesses. (Seek His blessing.) He can be pleased. (Trust Him.)

Turn your prayer into a statement of faith and take your stand against fear and uncertainty. Seek the God who can change your life and future in ways you could never do on your own.

*Life would be hopeless without You, Lord.
Believing that You exist and take care of me
allows me to trust You enough to stop hiding.*

EMBRACE THE NEW COLUMN

*You also were included in Christ when you heard
the message of truth, the gospel of your salvation.
When you believed, you were marked in him
with a seal, the promised Holy Spirit.*
EPHESIANS 1:13 NIV

The moment you trusted in Jesus and His ability to rescue you, He moved your name from lost to found, your life from old to new, and your condition from endangered to safe. You became part of God's family.

Your trust led you to pray, and that prayer declared your need and willingness to be rescued by God.

When you pray, remember that you can trust God with your heart, life, and future. . .as well as with the plans that He has made specifically for you. Prayer declares and promotes trust, and that trust transfers your name from the column of fear to the column of faith.

Because of Jesus' love, the power of fear in your Christian life has been neutralized.

*God, even though You want me to willingly
give You many things, the blessings You give
in return are so much better. Help me trust You
so that the things I fear seem less frightening.*

FEAR EXPELLED

[In God,] love has no fear, because perfect love expels all fear. If we are afraid, it is for fear of punishment, and this shows that we have not fully experienced his perfect love.
1 JOHN 4:18 NLT

Being expelled from a school or country means you can't return. Fear can be expelled, but unlike the other examples, it wants to keep crawling back. It wants you to miss it so much that you think you can't live without it.

God's love contains no fear. In fact, it expels fear, giving fear every reason to leave while giving you every reason to resist its return.

Fear tries to convince you that God is more interested in punishing you than in caring for you. This attitude can dent your relationship with God, ruining your faith and your ability to converse openly with Him.

Let His love expel your fear.

When I give You my faith, Father, take my fear away. I want Your love to transform my response and improve my conversations with You.

THE MORE YOU NOTICE

I remember the days of old; I meditate on all thy works; I muse on the work of thy hands.
PSALM 143:5 KJV

You've probably heard someone say, "What have you done for me lately?" King David wanted to remember what God *had* done for him, not just anticipate what He *was going to* do. If he could just spend enough time remembering God's goodness, the spotlight of grace would shrink all his difficulties.

Remembering was the vehicle; praise was the destination.

When life throws you the worst, it's easy to believe things will never get much better. But that's a perfect time to pray, blocking out your troubles and focusing solely on God's footprints. He's walked with you through every difficulty and caused the sun to rise on each new day. . .and then He's greeted you with an invitation to take yet another walk with Him. The more you look back at what God has done, the more you'll notice. . .and the more you notice, the more grateful you'll be.

Help me remember what You've done for me, Lord. Your help is worth celebrating.

THE SAME GOD

You know when I sit down or stand up. You know my thoughts even when I'm far away.
PSALM 139:2 NLT

The God you might have trouble remembering is the same God who knows what you had for breakfast last Thursday. He knows each time you stand up, even when you can't remember why or where you're going. He knows what you're thinking, even when you're daydreaming.

The same God who has been with you at every step has never made the decision to leave your side. In fact, God will always be by your side, unless you walk away. Don't do that!

The same God who has loved you still loves you. Try as hard as you want (which isn't advisable), but you can't make God stop loving you. His Son, Jesus, demonstrated that nothing can cut the cord of love between you and His heart.

The same God who created you wants to hear from you. You're never a bother to Him—even when you were broken, He bought you, rescuing you from the trouble you had found on your own.

This same God is amazing.

God, I want to remember that You have walked with me, are walking with me, and will always walk with me— and You do it because You love me.

PRAYER AND PRAISE

Is anyone among you in trouble? Let them pray.
Is anyone happy? Let them sing songs of praise.
JAMES 5:13 NIV

You get bad news. . .you pray. You get good news. . .you praise. There's always a reason to communicate with God. Whether your spirit is fractured and seemingly beyond repair, or your joy is exploding and you're not sure that your spirit can handle any more, God looks forward to both prayer and praise in the same divine conversation.

Show up with questions and leave with answers. Show up empty and leave filled. Show up broken and leave blessed. The most important step? Just show up.

Here's some great advice: you don't need a thank-you card or a fancy gift to show appreciation to God. Prayer and praise aren't just personal responses—they should be the responses of anyone God has rescued.

I will discover things that affect myself, my family, and my future—things I won't know how to handle. Bringing them to You is the only thing that makes sense, Father. Help me find the words to praise You for all You do.

FRUIT OF LIPS

A man shall be satisfied with good by the
fruit of his mouth: and the recompence of a
man's hands shall be rendered unto him.
PROVERBS 12:14 KJV

Your mouth can produce all kinds of messages. In Luke 6:45, Jesus describes your words as a harvest: "A good person produces good things from the treasury of a good heart, and an evil person produces evil things from the treasury of an evil heart. What you say flows from what is in your heart" (NLT). How pleased are you with your present crop?

What grows in the core of your being will eventually find its way to your mouth, no matter how hard you may try to hide it. When it reaches your lips, it gives a completely honest status report. That's why you can never make changes on your own. If you do not let God transform your heart, all you'll have is modified behavior—and your words will let you know when your efforts fail.

Let God's work inside you be the fruit of your mouth. He can succeed wherever you've struggled.

Lord, may I let You transform my words
and thoughts into something valuable.

FAITH REMINDS

*With my mouth I will greatly extol the L*ORD*; in the great throng of worshipers I will praise him.*
PSALM 109:30 NIV

Children often carry blankets with them for comfort. The blanket itself doesn't give them comfort—it is a symbol of the faith children have in their parents to help them in frightening situations.

Your faith is a gift given by God and backed by His promises. It represents your trust in Him. When you don't know how to deal with something, use that faith as a reminder that God can take care of your concerns.

Next, speak about what God did. Out loud. Around someone who'll listen. Brag about God, make Him famous, and celebrate His blessings. Take your good news to other Christians who can rejoice in your attitude of praise. Pray with others and let worship become the focus.

My faith is more than a security blanket, God.
It reminds me that You are trustworthy and that
You never fail. I could use that kind of reminder.

NEEDS WILL BE MET

I cried out to him for help, praising him as I spoke.
PSALM 66:17 NLT

Today's verse offers another example of needing help yet praising God before it arrives. This attitude is only possible when faith grips your life stronger than your circumstances do. Faith believes in a better outcome and God's perfect response, even when His delivery method doesn't match your expectations.

This response honors God because it declares that He is good and that His plans are perfect. The author of the verse was saying, "I need help. Thanks for helping me." But there's a deeper lesson: this plea was directed toward God and sprung from an emotionally compromised position. It was vocal and perhaps public.

Don't just believe—make sure unbelievers know that you believe. When you thank God publicly before His answer arrives, people will watch for your response and for God's deliverance. Faith tells a story that words can't capture, and others are willing to listen.

Make my faith story powerful, Lord. Not just because I trusted, but because You delivered.

AVERAGE. BLESSED. REMEMBERED.

"My heart rejoices in the LORD! The LORD has made me strong. Now I have an answer for my enemies; I rejoice because you rescued me."
1 SAMUEL 2:1 NLT

This was the prayer of a barren woman named Hannah. She cried out to God, praising Him all the while. She let her faith tell a story she could never write. She was fully convinced that God had a flawless plan.

God answered Hannah's prayer with a son named Samuel, whom He would one day use. And Hannah? She rejoiced. She was strengthened as her enemies were silenced. Hannah's heart was rescued.

You might think that God is interested only in certain types of people. These people seem different than you somehow. . .more blessed, perhaps. Yet many would consider Hannah an average woman who, if not for her faith, might've never been mentioned at all. Maybe that's a message for you: people will remember your life story when you ask God to show up.

Your faith makes God famous.

You're not just welcome in my story, God—You're needed. Make Yourself known to others through my faith in You.

FEAR AND WONDER

*[God's] mercy is on them that fear him
from generation to generation.*
LUKE 1:50 KJV

Some people fear God once and some fear Him twice, but these are different fears. When you haven't made the choice to follow God, it's only natural to be afraid. That's not surprising—you can also be afraid of people you've never met before. However, the fear dissipates when you spend time with the person you're afraid of.

But the Bible talks about a second kind of fear in relation to God. This fear is not equal to being afraid—it's a sense of awe and wonder. This fear will enhance your prayer life, making it easier for you to praise God. You can live with this fear for the rest of your life.

Everyone must make a choice about God, and many spend too much time being afraid of Him. But you don't need to be afraid of God when you know how wonderful He has always been.

*If I fear You today, Father, let it be the kind of fear
that knows You're wonderful, amazing, and inspiring.
Don't let me ever be afraid to talk to You.*

AWE EXCEEDED

You go before me and follow me. You place your hand of blessing on my head. Such knowledge is too wonderful for me, too great for me to understand!
PSALM 139:5–6 NLT

The way God works—His unexpected answers to prayer through divine appointments—is described as a mystery. King David said that God led the way before him, walked behind him to catch him when he stumbled, and stayed beside him as a companion willing to bless.

David, realizing he couldn't go anywhere to get away from God, proclaimed that God's knowledge and understanding exceeded any human capacity to think or feel. This is the God you pray to—the God who walks beside you and never leaves you. When you allow your mind to think through what this means, you can expect to be undone, overwhelmed, and filled with new reasons to worship.

God works in your circumstances. He can take bad things and make them good. He can take your broken chords and reorder them into a song of praise.

You pay incredible attention to me, Lord.
You know my needs, uncover my heart, and
walk with me. I don't deserve Your goodness,
but I never want to turn You away.

NO COMPARISONS

"There is no one holy like the LORD; there is no one besides you; there is no Rock like our God."
1 SAMUEL 2:2 NIV

Some websites help you comparison shop while buying a car. They tell you which car has the most powerful engine, the best gas mileage, and the best safety rating.

God isn't like a car. Try comparing His holiness with anyone else's. It can't be done. Who could accomplish what God has? No one. Who is stronger and more capable of keeping you safe? Stop looking. There's no one but God.

The God who made you is incomparable—no ninety-day trial required. There's no need for a money-back guarantee: you will not—cannot—find another option with the benefits God provides. The best you can hope for are unkept promises.

God never demands that you be religious. Instead, He asks that you develop a friendship with Him through prayer, allowing that friendship to change what you do, how you think, and what you believe.

I've always wanted to make sure I'm getting a good deal, God. That might work with things I can buy, but it doesn't work with You. I can't earn what You give freely. I'll never find a better offer.

CONFESS. REJOICE.

*I have rejoiced in the way of thy testimonies,
as much as in all riches.*
PSALM 119:14 KJV

Prayer should include confession. *Confession* means admitting you've done things that don't line up with God's instructions. You admit He was right in making the rules, and you learn what God wants so that you don't continue making the same bad decisions.

When people confess to the authorities, they tell all the details of what they did when breaking the law. Confession gets everything out in the open so that it can be dealt with.

God's laws (testimonies) are worth rejoicing about. You should be just as overjoyed with learning God's rules as you would be with locating a hidden treasure. But unlike hidden treasure, you can share God's treasure without losing any of it yourself. Confession brings a spiritual wealth of forgiveness and mercy, neither of which you can buy. They will always be a gift.

*I can trust You with my failures, Father. You take
the truth about me and use it to show me the truth
about You. You're just, but You love mercy. One day
You'll judge, but first You offer forgiveness. Keep
changing me until my failure is transformed.*

YOUR BEST INTEREST

If we confess our sins to him, he is faithful and just to
forgive us our sins and to cleanse us from all wickedness.
1 JOHN 1:9 NLT

God wants you to confess your sin. Why? Because you
need it. He offers it, but you must accept it.

You could choose not to confess, not to seek forgiveness, and not to pursue a clean heart—but how would that
benefit you? Confess and discover forgiveness. Admit God
is right and witness another miracle of God's faithfulness.
Admit you were wrong and be cleansed.

By admitting your sin, you're responding to what you
need the most. You're no longer pushing God away. You're
no longer trying to hide. You're running toward the only
One who's capable of connecting your present to the future
He's planned for you.

Confession is a gift to you, not a way of keeping God
informed. He already knows your condition. Do you?

Without confession in my prayer life, I can
only walk with a limp. Even though You're
walking forward, I'll never be sure of my next
step until I'm honest with You, Lord.

HE STANDS UP FOR YOU

For there is one God and one mediator between God and mankind, the man Christ Jesus.
1 Timothy 2:5 niv

If prayer can be defined as a conversation with God, then Jesus prays for you when He talks to God on your behalf. When does Jesus do that? Whenever you sin and then confess.

There's one God, and you answer to Him for every sin you commit. However, He loves you so much that He sent His Son, Jesus, to be penalized for your sin. That was His gift to you.

Now that the penalty has been paid and accepted by God, you can either accept or reject the payment. If you accept it, the One who paid the penalty also acts as a defense lawyer when you sin. His firm legal opinion when you confess your sin is that you're no longer guilty.

Forgiveness eliminates all charges against you, bringing you back into a relationship with God. The Savior who paid the penalty for your sin stands with you as well.

You made it possible for me to be free, God. Your Son didn't come to make my life harder, but easier. He forgives. He defends. He loves.

SIN NOT

My little children, these things write I unto you, that ye sin not. And if any man sin, we have an advocate with the Father, Jesus Christ the righteous.
1 John 2:1 KJV

Today's verse restates what you learned yesterday: Jesus defends you before God. But there are three key additions in this passage, all in the first sentence.

My little children: John was addressing young Christians—individuals who had a lot to learn but also possessed the childlike trust that Jesus commended. They broke God's laws but sought their heavenly Daddy.

These things I write: They needed to be reminded that help was available. They needed to know they didn't have to remain in a self-imposed state of conviction.

Sin not: This last item on the list of new information may seem obvious, but among the children of the faith it is worth repeating—sin not.

The first half of this verse encourages us to stay away from sin—to reject its influence. But when you do sin, don't hesitate. Run to God, telling Him what happened and what you did.

It would be easy to just live for Your forgiveness, Father, but that would discount Your command to obey. Help me grow while I remember Your instruction to "sin not."

CLARITY

Thy word is a lamp unto my feet,
and a light unto my path.
PSALM 119:105 KJV

Your vision's been getting a little blurry, and someone recommends you get an eye exam. You don't think it's a big deal though. It hasn't really stopped you from living life and doing what you love. Even when the optometrist says you need glasses, you ask for a second opinion. You deny there's an issue or think it's just temporary. But when you wear glasses for the first time, you're surprised with how clear everything has become.

The same can be said about your spiritual vision. You can believe you know exactly where you need to go, but God offers a degree of clarity that you can find only through constant communication with Him.

God's clarity may only reveal enough of your future for you to map out one step at a time, but that'll be enough to move you from where you are into someplace much better.

I've already lived long enough to know that my plans
have not moved me to a clearer place, Lord. Maybe
this is the place where Your lamp and light can give
me a perfect answer for my next step questions.

OBEDIENCE

Don't just listen to God's word. You must do what it says. Otherwise, you are only fooling yourselves.
JAMES 1:22 NLT

You can hear what God has said, find it interesting, yet still not consider it revolutionary enough to change your actions. You can hear God's message without believing God said it. You can hear God's Word and never recognize His voice.

Even when you listen to what He says, there are two ways you can still find yourself in trouble: (1) by believing what you've learned is merely good information and (2) by believing no action (obedience) is required.

You might think that obedience is a good idea—as long as you can put it off into the future. Provided you don't have to obey today, it seems admirable to say that someday you should.

You should ask God to help you hear His voice and do what He knows is best for you. Obedience will not deny you a meaningful life—it will provide meaning for the life God has given you.

Let there be some urgency in my obedience, God. I don't want to assume You're okay with my delay. Open my eyes to see ways to obey.

REAFFIRMED

"But I, with shouts of grateful praise, will sacrifice to you. What I have vowed I will make good. I will say, 'Salvation comes from the LORD.'"
JONAH 2:9 NIV

It's easy to criticize Jonah for running the other way when God gave him a job. Who does that? Well, you do—or at least you will.

The Bible is filled with imperfect people who are used by a perfect God. These examples exist to show that personal struggles do not disqualify us from God's love and His work in our lives.

Don't fall into the habit of contrasting yourself against these imperfect examples. You might think you wouldn't do what they did, but you're only human, just as they were.

When reading stories of people who sinned, focus on what they learned and how God dealt with them. In Jonah's case, he learned to communicate with God without arguing. His prayer reaffirmed his commitment to trust and obey God. He turned from rejecting God's plan to honoring God for His ability to rescue.

When I fail, I will discover that You're a faithful Father. Help me read Your examples to realize that what I experience is common and that You haven't abandoned me.

A FREEDOM PRAYER

Moses prayed for the people.
NUMBERS 21:7 KJV

There was a generation of Israelites who knew only slavery. . .so they acted like slaves. When God brought freedom, they grew uncomfortable. They had watched their Egyptian masters serve various non-gods, so they themselves ventured away from God frequently. As a result, snakes began biting them, sickening many and killing a few. The people asked Moses for help.

Moses knew that God had the answer, so he prayed for the people. Once again, God brought freedom to His slavery-prone children. It wasn't the first or last time God would intervene for them—they had to learn and relearn that freedom comes from God alone.

You can pray for your family, friends, coworkers, and neighbors, asking God to intervene when trouble visits them. And it's not just a one-time prayer. As you pray again and again, your prayer life will thrive because it includes others.

You brought people into my life for a reason, Lord.
Give me the wisdom to recognize their needs and
to pray for them, even if they don't ask for it.
Give them the freedom You've offered me.

GOD WILL LISTEN

*The LORD was angry enough with Aaron to destroy
him, but at that time I prayed for Aaron too.*
DEUTERONOMY 9:20 NIV

When Moses walked up the mountain alone, God met him
there and gave him the Ten Commandments. Meanwhile,
Aaron, Moses' brother, stayed with the people at the base
of the mountain. They were getting restless and no longer
recognized God as their leader, so they brought gold to
Aaron and convinced him to sculpt a calf. The people then
accepted his sculpture as their new divine leader.

God had just told Moses that the people should have
no other god but Him, and now Aaron stood guilty of helping the people break that command. Once again, Moses
prayed on another's behalf—this time for his brother. God
listened to Moses.

It would be wonderful if everyone could read God's
instructions and follow them consistently, but that just
doesn't happen. So pray for others. Encourage them to pray
for you. Stand in the gap between those you love and the
God who cares. You can be sure God will listen.

*Where I am in my faith is not where others are, God.
They are either farther along or lagging behind. May they
pray for me. May I pray for them. May we keep walking.*

DON'T BE A HINDRANCE

They buried the bones of Saul and his son Jonathan in the tomb of Saul's father Kish, at Zela in Benjamin, and did everything the king commanded. After that, God answered prayer in behalf of the land.
2 Samuel 21:14 niv

Saul was the first king of Israel, but he was not a good one. He started off well, but jealousy and envy led him to decisions that harmed himself, his family, and all Israel. God wasn't pleased with the king, and everyone suffered.

However, once this rebellious king's life was over, God began answering the people's prayers. Disobedience comes at a price, especially for those who refuse to seek God. That price sometimes extends to others.

The absence of a prayer life can amplify your feelings of loneliness and helplessness. Saul did not seek God's guidance or lead his nation spiritually, so his reign was ineffective and filled with bloodshed, revenge, and disobedience.

Seek God, relieve fear, accept love, and follow hard.

I want to be a good example of someone who follows You, Father. When I don't follow, I can't lead anyone to You. I don't want to hinder anyone's prayers.

NO ONE LIKE HIM

*Lord God of Israel, there is no God like thee,
in heaven above, or on earth beneath, who keepest
covenant and mercy with thy servants that walk
before thee with all their heart.*
1 Kings 8:23 KJV

King Solomon would have remembered the stories of how Saul had hunted David, Solomon's father, and how God had rejected Saul because of his violent impulses. King David had not been perfect, but he had made prayer a priority—an example that Solomon, the wisest king who ever lived, observed and followed.

Solomon concluded that no one is like God, who keeps His promises and shows mercy to all who walk with Him. This wasn't a rehearsed bedtime prayer. This was years of experience blossoming into wisdom—and it was written down for your benefit.

Whether you lead or follow, the outcomes of your decisions will significantly improve whenever you honestly and vocally proclaim that no one is, ever has been, or ever will be like God.

*Lord, thank You for listening to me like no one
else does. May I seek You with all my heart.*

MOUNTAINTOP PROOF

At the usual time for offering the evening sacrifice, Elijah the prophet walked up to the altar and prayed, "O LORD, God of Abraham, Isaac, and Jacob, prove today that you are God in Israel and that I am your servant. Prove that I have done all this at your command."
1 KINGS 18:36 NLT

Elijah the prophet prayed that it would not rain. Three years later, that prayer was still being answered. To prove that God was worth following, Elijah confronted the wicked King Ahab, who had been following something less.

On a mountaintop, the priests of the non-god Baal built altars, then danced, prayed, and injured themselves trying to get their god's attention. They needed him to send fire from heaven to consume their sacrifice, but nothing happened.

Then Elijah prayed the prayer at the top of this page, knowing God would answer. God was about to prove His existence and superiority, exposing Baal for the non-god that he was. Suddenly, something happened: God sent fire.

This same powerful God is the One you can pray to right now!

I am amazed when I read stories of your greatness, God. Help me trust that You're using the same power today to work for my good.

CALMING A SERVANT

Elisha prayed, "Open his eyes, Lord, so that he may see." Then the Lord opened the servant's eyes, and he looked and saw the hills full of horses and chariots of fire all around Elisha.
2 Kings 6:17 niv

Imagine the faith it would take to speak a nine-word prayer and know God would answer. Elisha had that kind of faith.

The Israelites were at war with the Arameans, and anyone who saw the battlefield would have said Israel was losing. . .anyone except Elisha. Even though his servant was terrified, Elisha knew everything would be fine. "'What shall we do?' the servant asked" (6:15 niv). In response, Elisha prayed. The servant then had the rare honor of seeing God at work in ways most eyes can't see.

You may never know how, but you can be positive that God is working things out in your life. Let that be enough. Elisha prayed nine words, but sometimes, all you have to pray is one word—Help—and God will answer it just the same.

Be confident in the God who answers prayer.

You are never low on supplies or short on ideas, Father. Help me trust Your direction and believe Your goodness.

RECOGNIZING GREATNESS

Hezekiah prayed before the LORD, and said, O LORD God of Israel, which dwellest between the cherubims, thou art the God, even thou alone, of all the kingdoms of the earth; thou hast made heaven and earth. LORD, bow down thine ear, and hear: open, LORD, thine eyes, and see: and hear the words of Sennacherib, which hath sent him to reproach the living God.
2 KINGS 19:15–16 KJV

Hezekiah, the thirteenth king of Judah, was also one of the best. He loved God, served Him, and prayed to Him. But his faith was put to the test when the rogue nation of Assyria encompassed Judah in a fear-based attack.

Sennacherib, a representative from Assyria, openly proclaimed to the people that no nation had ever stood against Assyria successfully. It was in their best interest, he suggested, to give up before Judah was ravaged by war.

However, instead of gathering more troops or asking other nations to help, Hezekiah prayed. Recognizing God's greatness, he invited God to examine Sennacherib's words and respond. God answered the king's prayer by rescuing the people of Judah.

We often pray after strategizing or taking stock of our personal resources, Lord. Help my prayer to arrive much sooner.

NO WORST-CASE SCENARIO

"O Lord, God of our ancestors, you alone are the God who is in heaven. You are ruler of all the kingdoms of the earth. You are powerful and mighty; no one can stand against you!"
2 Chronicles 20:6 NLT

Jehoshaphat, king of Judah, believed in the power of prayer. He accepted his role as a leader who prayed with, in front of, and for his people.

Where others saw war, Jehoshaphat saw God's plan unfolding. One day, a man named Jahaziel told the king he had a message from God: "Do not be afraid! Don't be discouraged by this mighty army, for the battle is not yours, but God's" (20:15 NLT).

The king was right in saying that no one could stand against a powerful and mighty God. He spoke truth when he praised God as ruler over every kingdom on earth. He was wise in proclaiming that God is without comparison.

Never allow your circumstances to lie to you about God's goodness.

God, just because I am sometimes overwhelmed doesn't mean that You are. When all I can see are worst-case scenarios, remind me that You have the best ideas.

A GOD TESTIMONY

So we fasted and petitioned our God about this, and he answered our prayer.
EZRA 8:23 NIV

The Israelites had been exiled in Babylon for decades, and Ezra was one of the first to return to the land God had promised. He could have asked the Babylonian king, Artaxerxes, for soldiers to protect those traveling back to their home, but instead, Ezra encouraged the people to focus on God and pray diligently for protection—without the aid of pagan soldiers.

Ezra wanted the people to see that God could be trusted, and the trip away from Babylon would be the perfect basis for such a profound testimony.

What experience have you had that would've been a failure without God's intervention? Why was His help the only possible answer? How has that encouraged you to share your story with others?

Those who believe in God and pray to Him often will likely see Him working behind the scenes, managing even their most difficult situations.

When I face trials and feel as if my world will fall apart without Your help, please show up, Father. I can't rescue myself, and I don't want to be rescued by anyone but You.

PERSONAL CRISIS

When I heard these words. . .I sat down and
wept, and mourned certain days, and fasted,
and prayed before the God of heaven.
NEHEMIAH 1:4 KJV

A lot of powerful movies have been made about people whose personal crises—be it the loss of a farm, the destruction of a home in a tornado, or another such catastrophe—led them into a place of resolution. But such stories are not just for theatrical release.

Like Ezra and most of his fellow Israelites, Nehemiah was a prisoner in Babylon. He worked for the king, but his story truly began when he learned about the plight of the few Israelites who had returned to Jerusalem. They were being disgraced by people who didn't want them to return, the city walls had been burned, and the city was in near ruin.

The news broke his heart and moved him to prayer.

Love can do that to a man. Often, life-shattering catastrophes can convince you to make foolish decisions. . .or they can lead you to pray to the God who rebuilds walls.

Rebuild relationships, Lord. Rebuild what's broken.
Prepare the way. Point my feet in Your direction.

THE PRAYER DECISION

*When Daniel learned that the law had been signed,
he went home and knelt down as usual in his upstairs
room, with its windows open toward Jerusalem.
He prayed three times a day, just as he had
always done, giving thanks to his God.*
DANIEL 6:10 NLT

No one was more important to Daniel than God. Don't
misunderstand: Daniel didn't disrespect or verbally abuse
other people, and he never refused a reasonable request
from the king. But when a new law that prohibited prayer
was enacted, Daniel refused to budge.

Three times a day, Daniel spent time conversing with
God. It was the source of his honor and strength—his con-
duit of encouragement.

To Daniel, prayer was a habit he'd had for most of his
life. It was very important, and it helped more people than
it could ever hurt. It was rooted in the law of love, and no
one could outlaw that.

*I don't want prayer to be optional, God. Let it be so
important to me that I could never do without it.*

WORTH THE ISOLATION

In the morning, rising up a great while before day, he went out, and departed into a solitary place, and there prayed.
MARK 1:35 KJV

Group prayer has its time and place. It's uplifting and God encourages it. But Jesus showed the other side of the prayer coin. He knew that His best conversations with God would happen in a quiet time and in a quiet place, so He chose to pray at morning, while most people still slept, in a solitary place without distractions.

You can pray anywhere and anytime. You don't have to choose the early morning or late night. You don't have to go to a mountain or a vast wilderness. God is always available. However, this verse seems to suggest that some prayers are worth subtracting your distractions to add concentration. An undivided heart often results in multiplied blessings.

Prayer is that important. So as you pray, use your heart, mind, soul, and strength to intentionally connect with God.

I don't want to settle only for "side of the road" prayers, Lord. Help me find the right destination to connect my heart to Yours.

COURAGE IN
THE CONVERSATION

Going a little farther, he fell with his face to the ground and prayed, "My Father, if it is possible, may this cup be taken from me. Yet not as I will, but as you will."
MATTHEW 26:39 NIV

Jesus fought temptation, faced trials, and got hungry. He experienced what you experience, and He made tough choices to follow God's plan. If He had failed, He wouldn't have been perfect. And if He hadn't been perfect, His sacrifice would've been meaningless. And if it were meaningless, there would be no rescue plan. And if there is no rescue plan, you have no hope.

God's Son was facing something He'd never experienced before—death by crucifixion. Jesus was not looking forward to dying on a cross; in fact, He even wondered if there was any way to avoid it. But Jesus prayed with an end goal in mind. He wanted God's will to prevail.

Jesus' short prayer (that He prayed more than once) can give you the courage to follow, even when walking the other way seems easier. His example provides the strength you need to make it through hard days.

Father, give me a heart that longs for You, a soul that speaks with You, and a life well lived for You.

LISTENING

Around midnight Paul and Silas were praying and singing hymns to God, and the other prisoners were listening.
ACTS 16:25 NLT

Being unjustly imprisoned would lead most people into anger, despair, or violence. But as others slept, Paul and Silas were not yelling for justice or plotting revenge—they were praying and singing.

There's more to the story, and God would later show up for these two, but let's focus on this verse alone.

This duo experienced a personal worship service that was attended by a captive audience. The other prisoners couldn't leave, but they never told the two men to be quiet. On the contrary, they "were listening."

It would have been easy to ridicule these hymn singers or to question where God was when they prayed. But as the two innocent men spent the night with the convicted, the convicted began listening to their message of hope.

When life seems unfair, may my life reflect You, God. When justice seems to pass me by, may I pray and praise, letting those who don't know You see a difference in my response.

YOUR TIME OUT

*But thou, when thou prayest, enter into thy closet,
and when thou hast shut thy door, pray to thy
Father which is in secret; and thy Father which
seeth in secret shall reward thee openly.*
MATTHEW 6:6 KJV

There's something powerful about going to a place where
you expect to meet with God. As you gradually feel more
comfortable in this place, you can become emotionally connected to it. It can remove distractions, inviting a
more concentrated time with God. Such a place has been
called a prayer closet or war room. It's where you can take
a timeout.

The reason for shutting the door is to minimize distractions. This kind of prayer is a private, personal, and
authentic conversation between the Creator and His much-
loved creation. It's not a showcase for lofty vocabulary. It's
a personal space for vulnerable expression.

God can meet with you anywhere, but perhaps some
things can only be shared with Him in this private, comforting place.

*Sometimes, I need to travel away from the noise
to be in Your presence, Lord. Help me find a
memorable place for my conversations with You.*

VASTLY SUPERIOR

Rescue me from my enemies, Lord;
I run to you to hide me.
PSALM 143:9 NLT

This is the kind of plea that's meant for that secluded place of personal prayers. David prayed this because he was being pursued by those who wanted to harm him. He needed a rescue plan, but he was either out of ideas or smart enough to know that God's plans were vastly superior to anything he could dream up.

David was wise enough to know that God's presence offered the greatest security. He was bold enough to ask for help, and he was humble enough to recognize that God did the rescuing. And each story that sprung from David's private time with God, he would share to encourage someone like you.

King David didn't have to wait to see if his plan would work—he simply ducked out of society and took counsel with God. When he returned, he was able to share God's faithfulness with people who needed His rescue.

Make me wise enough to run to You, Father. Make me bold enough to share my deepest struggle. Make me strong enough to continually walk with You.

STRONG ENOUGH TO CARRY

Trust in him at all times, you people; pour out your hearts to him, for God is our refuge.
PSALM 62:8 NIV

Why do you go to God when trouble visits? If you didn't trust God, you wouldn't go to Him. What'd be the point if you didn't think He can help? You wouldn't think of Him as a refuge, and your burdens couldn't be lightened because you wouldn't be close to anyone strong enough to carry them.

Can your spiritual life thrive if you only trust God's goodness occasionally? No. You should never stop trusting God's ability and willingness to help.

Allow God to turn your heart upside down and pour out all the muck. You might be keeping it for emergency use, but how has it ever helped you? What does hauling your burdens around do for you?

Trust God today, and never quit. Be authentic in your conversations with Him, confident that He is forever trust-worthy.

May I always offer my trust as an every-moment gift to You, God. May I accept the protection and rescue that You offer.

PEOPLE OF LIGHT

*Once you were full of darkness, but now you have
light from the Lord. So live as people of light!*
Ephesians 5:8 nlt

You were once a baby, but now you're a man. . .so live like
one. You were once a kindergartener, but now you're much
more mature. . .so be a lifelong learner. You were once fed
from a bottle, but now you have teeth. . .so start eating solid
food. You were born as one thing, but God created you to
be something more. So be something more.

It makes no sense to live like you've learned nothing.
As a Christian, you can look back and remember the fear
you had when you didn't know what to do next. But you're
learning, so stop running back to the fear you've left behind.
You represent God's light, so stop retreating into darkness,
where it's easy to lose your way.

You're becoming a new creation, so resist the urge to
run back to what's familiar. Knock it off!

*I often run back into darkness instead of living in
Your light, Lord. Help me resist the temptation to
return to something that has always brought failure.*

WHAT TO ASK FOR

Jabez cried out to the God of Israel, "Oh, that you would bless me and enlarge my territory! Let your hand be with me, and keep me from harm so that I will be free from pain." And God granted his request.
1 CHRONICLES 4:10 NIV

What if your prayers matched God's heart so well that He already wanted to answer them? Knowing what God wants can help you learn what to ask for and what to avoid.

Jabez's prayer seems simple, specific, and bold. . .maybe even a bit presumptuous. Yet God answered it.

You should never assume that God's response will be better if you are bossy and demanding. The intensity of Jabez's cry to God indicates he was passionate about his request. Maybe he spent a lot of time deliberating on it before he uttered the words.

It's clear that Jabez followed God and that his request matched God's heart. How do we know this? God answered his prayer.

Father, may my prayers reflect what I'm learning from Your Word. May I read so that You can teach. Only then will our conversations be more understandable.

ASK HIM

Seek the LORD and his strength, seek his face continually.
1 CHRONICLES 16:11 KJV

God is a great listener. Do you talk to Him, or do you expect Him just to give you something you've never asked for? Maybe you want Him to come to your rescue. . .but you've never asked to be rescued. Or perhaps you want Him to fulfill a need. . .but you've failed to tell Him that you need it. What kind of logic is that? God has no obligation to answer un-prayed prayers.

God supplied the Bible so that you can always hear from Him. So even though He knows everything about you, He still wants you to share your heart with Him in prayer.

Chase God. Ask Him to help. Have conversations with Him as often as you can.

Don't think you're doing God a favor by not asking for His help—you're actually holding His answer at arm's length. God is not small, and His resources have no limits. His mercy is a healing spiritual salve.

Here's some logic: God created the universe, so He can help you. Ask.

Let me never hesitate to call Your name, God.
Help me know You so well that I can talk to
You without a hint of awkwardness.

YOUR NEXT BEST MOVE

But God did listen! He paid attention to my prayer.
PSALM 66:19 NLT

King David, who most scholars believe wrote this psalm, faced enormous adversity. He didn't always make perfect choices, but when he obeyed God and then offered up a prayer, God listened.

Many people think that God is unapproachable and distant. But given that God is the One who holds the world and all its inhabitants together, it seems reasonable to assume He is always close and attentive.

If you were to create a documentary on whether God answers prayer, you wouldn't need to look far to find His faithfulness dotting your own storyline—even if you lacked the statistics. The further you look back, the more your stories would accumulate. Soon, your documentary would transform into a series and then into a lifelong story of divine dependability.

God has listened, He is listening, and He will never stop listening—so prayer will always be your next, best move.

I've been gathering facts, Lord, and I've found that You pay attention to Your family's needs. Help me believe that You hear me when I pray and that Your answers are best for me.

FAITHFUL WITH A REASON

If we are faithless, he remains faithful,
for he cannot disown himself.
2 Timothy 2:13 niv

You might think that you need to be perfect before you can seek God. But that's not true. He wants you to know *He* is perfect, and that's the only reason you *can* approach Him.

People probably feel the urge to be perfect before talking with God because that's how human interactions work. When you went on your first date, you likely did everything you could to impress her. You tried to say and do the right things, and you paid attention to her. You hid your faults and did your best not to let them show up in front of her.

You can't keep that pace up in dating or in other relationships, and neither can you when praying to God. You'll need His help—and He's guaranteed that He'll always be faithful. You don't need to put on an act to impress Him. He doesn't have to put on an act to impress us.

Maybe the best result of Your constant faithfulness,
Father, is that I can be certain that You have
never abandoned me—and You never will.

THE WAY OUT

*The temptations in your life are no different from
what others experience. And God is faithful. He will
not allow the temptation to be more than you can
stand. When you are tempted, he will show you
a way out so that you can endure.*
1 CORINTHIANS 10:13 NLT

If you want to compare yourself to others, this might be one of the best verses to use. Are you tempted? Yes. Are other people tempted? Yes. So if temptation is the measurement, you're on a level playing field with everyone you meet.

God, on the other hand, isn't tempted. He's never sinned. He doesn't tempt anyone; instead, He offers a way out, because temptation is practically impossible to resist on your own. You'll nearly always fail.

Temptation is like a house of mirrors—you know there's a way out, but you can't find it. God is the only One who can lead you through the confusion to the other side. So when temptation shows up again, start by praying for His help.

*I'm convinced that You can lead me
through temptation, God. Give me enough
wisdom to ask for directions.*

GOD'S CONTRACT WITH YOU

What if some were unfaithful? Will their unfaithfulness nullify God's faithfulness?
ROMANS 3:3 NIV

You've probably been critical of people who claim to follow God but still make questionable choices. Comparing yourself to them might boost your self-esteem, but it won't solve the deeper issue—your disappointment. Because you serve a faithful God, you probably expected more from His followers.

Because people are human, failure is inevitable. So pray for others—they could use the extra strength. You should also know that sin can never nullify God's contract with someone. His contract is faithful, even when no one else is.

Psalm 146:3 says it best: "Do not put your trust in princes, in human beings, who cannot save" (NIV). God asks you only to trust Him, to love Him, and to love others. Nothing anyone can do can change God's faithfulness to you.

Don't allow me to be jaded when others let me down, Lord. Loving others allows me to forgive them. Trusting You allows me to hope. Let me hope unrestrainedly.

BEYOND YOUR REACH

Thy mercy, O LORD, is in the heavens; and thy faithfulness reacheth unto the clouds.
PSALM 36:5 KJV

Writers can never give superheroes unlimited power. Why? There would be no suspense. You'd know the outcome of every encounter. No one could even challenge them. They would never experience jeopardy because they could never lose.

As a Christian, you serve a God who has unlimited power. There's no need to sit on the edge of your seat, anxious about an outcome. God can't lose. He can't be challenged. He's never in jeopardy. Find comfort in knowing that even your worst experiences are subject to God's power at work in your life.

But even with all this strength, God still invites you to talk to Him anytime, anywhere. Because He loves you, He'll always listen to you and act in your best interest.

God is stronger than your imperfection and wiser than your greatest revelation. He's God—there is no other. No suspense.

Keep me from thinking You're not interested in me, Father. Your strength keeps me and Your love carries me, even when I'm sure I cannot take another step.

WAYWARD NO MORE

*"For I know the plans I have for you," says the L*ORD.
*"They are plans for good and not for disaster, to give you
a future and a hope. In those days when you pray, I will
listen. If you look for me wholeheartedly, you will find me."*
JEREMIAH 29:11–13 NLT

These verses were written to wayward Israelites who'd rejected God, running when they should have stayed with Him and staying when He invited them to follow.

Yet God had a good and trustworthy plan for His people that would map out their future and keep them from disaster—but the people still walked away. Even then, God said that the people would one day rediscover prayer. When they sought God diligently from a place of pain and awkwardness, they would find Him.

While this passage was written for the Israelites, it contains universal truths. You might abandon God, but God never abandons you. When you search for Him, He will be found.

*Help me seek You, God. Help me
find You and discover hope.*

HE'S GOT YOU

*Because of the L*ORD*'s great love we are not consumed,
for his compassions never fail. They are new every
morning; great is your faithfulness.*
LAMENTATIONS 3:22–23 NIV

If your sin were a fire, you would be consumed. But God's love puts those fires out. And this isn't just a one-time offer—He can rescue you every day from the choices you make. His compassion is fresh and available before you even open your eyes each morning.

When you find yourself breaking God's laws again, ask God to rescue you. Don't sit smoldering in your own fire— don't be consumed. God freely offers His help, so don't be too proud to ask or too stubborn to accept it. You'll always lose if you do.

God's love and compassion are endless. There's never been a spiritual power outage. No generators are needed, and no downtime has ever been logged. When you have Him, He's got you.

*I need You, Lord. Sometimes, I feel like I'm
being consumed, so thanks for reminding
me that Your love and compassion protect
me from the heat of my own sin*

PRAY. PRAISE. PROCLAIM.

———————

I have not hid thy righteousness within my heart;
I have declared thy faithfulness and thy salvation:
I have not concealed thy lovingkindness and
thy truth from the great congregation.
PSALM 40:10 KJV

The words you pray reveal your level of gratitude, and that thankfulness can overflow into everyday conversations about God's goodness and what He has accomplished in your life.

King David said that these topics weren't hidden in the vault of his heart. He spoke openly of God's faithfulness and righteousness, acting with full disclosure. He revealed God's truth and lovingkindness to those who knew, those who didn't, and those who should have known. This wasn't private praise—it was public and purposeful.

You can hide the truth about God's goodness, or you can follow David's example and share it through prayer, praise, and proclamation. God is good—let people hear that from you.

Why is it easy to hide the truth about You, Father?
Why would I deny that I know You just to impress total
strangers? Prevent my lips from making this mistake.

WHEN SAME MAKES A DIFFERENCE

Jesus Christ is the same yesterday, today, and forever.
HEBREWS 13:8 NLT

Take a pencil, jam it into a sharpener, and watch it emerge with a finer point. Suddenly, it's useful for conveying ideas, assembling thoughts, and sharing your heart.

Use today's verse to do some similar sharpening. Take all your rough, crusty, truth-blunting thoughts and sharpen them with God's Word. Discover that Jesus is the same yesterday, today, and forever. At no point in human history has He ever considered changing. His love for you has never changed, wavered, or delayed.

Everything you've been learning has been sharpening this point. When can you trust Him? Always. When is He unfaithful? Never. Write yourself a note and keep it handy. Write it in a card and send it. Write it on your heart. . .and let others read it.

This is a big point that has taken several days to develop: God is faithful. He always has been, and He always will be. His Son is equally as faithful. You can't change Him, and He won't let Himself be changed.

Between the two of us, God, I'm the only one who needs changing. So change me. Help me believe and trust in You.

HOLY AND BLAMELESS

*For he chose us in him before the creation of the
world to be holy and blameless in his sight.*
EPHESIANS 1:4 NIV

God, who never changes, has always loved you. He's the
same God who made a plan for your future before He created the earth. He doesn't want just to watch you grow up
and see how you do on your own. He wants to help you.
He created you to reflect Him. He wants you to move from
sinful and guilty to holy and blameless. But you don't find
holiness and perfection in yourself—God transfers it to
your spiritual account. Once God forgives your sins, you
are blameless in His sight.

Follow this chain of events: Before you were born, God
knew you, chose you, and planned for you to have a holy
and blameless life. He then sent Jesus to take away your
guiltiness. Now, all you have to do is confess your sins to
Him and accept His finished work.

*Always remind me that You made it possible
for me to accept your perfection, Lord,
even when I don't feel like I can.*

SEARCHED AND RESCUED

O lord, thou hast searched me, and known me.
PSALM 139:1 KJV

Here's something you might struggle to believe: you don't just *know* that God searches you and knows everything about you—you *want* Him to.

Wickedness is an invader that can dominate your thoughts and actions, but God can uncover it by searching your heart, mind, and soul. Yet this is like a game of hide and seek—you hide; God seeks. Once God diagnoses the problem, He can fix it. So by wanting Him to track down whatever has invaded your life, you're asking for His help in eradicating what doesn't belong.

Let God perform a spiritual physical on you. Ask Him to tell you what's hindering your spiritual growth, and let Him offer a prescription. Apply God's wisdom and resources to your needs to improve your spiritual health.

Search me and know what needs Your help,
Father. Examine my heart and eliminate
whatever bends it away from You. Give me a
plan for recovery that keeps me close to You.

IN THE HEART VAULT

I have hidden your word in my heart,
that I might not sin against you.
PSALM 119:11 NLT

Because wickedness and deceitfulness like to invade your heart, God has given you a way to displace these distractions. If you don't want to break God's rules, you should know what those rules are. You'll find them in the Bible.

A man's prayers become more powerful after he reads God's Word. If you don't read His Word, your conversations with Him aren't just one-sided—they're entirely self-centered. You're telling God that your needs are important and His commands are not.

When you read God's commands, think about them and hide them in your heart vault—that'll give you the highest chance of obeying His rules. Then you'll have no excuse because you'll know what He wants you to do.

As you ponder the importance of His rules, you'll discover that the same God who gave the rules can also help you keep them.

Your words help me learn how to speak to You, God.
I want to know You so well that I no longer have the
questions I would have asked without Your Word.

A GIFT UNEXPECTED

*It shall come to pass, that before they call, I will answer;
and while they are yet speaking, I will hear.*
ISAIAH 65:24 KJV

For a person who doubts whether God hears and answers prayer, there may still be some value in prayer. Call it a therapeutic experience, spending time reviewing the day and then passing that information on to no one in particular.

Yet those who are convinced God is real and are willing to talk with Him often share an unusual bit of news: God answered the prayer before it was even prayed. It doesn't always happen that way, but when it does, it's a potent reminder that God has always known what you need. He even knows how He's going to supply it.

God did that for the Israelites, and He does it for you. This gift of grace reminds you that you are part of His family. . .and that He loves giving you unexpected gifts.

*I've never done anything to earn Your compassion,
Lord, but I've still received it. Thank You for Your gifts
that invite me closer and persuade me to stay.*

SO MANY QUESTIONS

*Take delight in the Lord, and he will
give you your heart's desires.*
PSALM 37:4 NLT

Taking God's Word out of context is easy. For instance, you can cut off the first part of the verse above and claim, "The Bible says God will give me my heart's desires!" That's true, but it's only half the story. Many would love to believe that God will give them anything they want. But does this verse really teach that?

Before your prayers can be answered, you have a responsibility: "Take delight in the Lord." What does taking delight look like? Does it mean living however you want? If you take delight in the Lord, will you skip prayer and neglect the Bible, or will you embrace these activities like close friends?

Does following God change what your heart desires? If so, how?

Consider these questions when wondering how your delight in God connects with your desires in life. The first delight changes the second.

*I can be shortsighted when I pray to You,
Father. When my desires are not rooted in
You, I will make immature requests. Grow my
connection to You before I ask for anything.*

FUTURE FAMILIARITY

You discern my going out and my lying down;
you are familiar with all my ways.
PSALM 139:3 NIV

It is amazing how many people think life is totally uncontrolled. Such a worldview would cause anxiety. But God is familiar with everything that everyone says and does—whether they follow Him or not. The morning news is never news to God.

A headline you read may alter your circumstances. . .but not your future. God's familiarity with each one of us means life is not just a string of random events leading to an uncertain outcome. Stay in constant communication with Him and watch as He bends all your circumstances—even the bad ones—to align your future with His perfect plan.

Fear is never necessary (or desirable) for followers of Jesus. He and His Father have everything well in hand. Just ask for peace.

Take my bad news and bend it toward the future
You've planned for me, God. Thanks for being so
familiar with me. Help me trust Your redirection.

ALL NIGHT LONG

How precious also are thy thoughts unto me,
O God! how great is the sum of them! If I should
count them, they are more in number than the
sand: when I awake, I am still with thee.
PSALM 139:17–18 KJV

If you have children, you might pray with them before they go to bed. Rest comes easier for them when you're the last person they see before they sleep. They're reassured of your presence and love.

Similarly, when you pray to the God who thinks about you, you can go to sleep trusting Him to calm your concerns. Be reassured of God's presence and love—He'll still be with you in the morning.

God doesn't wander off when you're sleeping; He looks after you when you're awake and when your body is at rest. God thinks about you—a lot. Because He wants the best for you, He stays close, encouraging you with confidence and comfort on your journey.

Stay close, Lord. Keep watch while I rest.
Give me the courage to sleep, and then greet me
in the morning and walk with me once more.

GRACE PRAISE

So we praise God for the glorious grace he has poured out on us who belong to his dear Son.
EPHESIANS 1:6 NLT

You've come this far—by now you should realize that God wants to be your friend. He prefers closeness, and He's given you no reason to avoid Him. He wants to help you understand how to walk forward into the future He's planned for you.

When you pray, take some time to acknowledge His assistance. If you belong to Jesus, His Son, He's poured out His grace on you, lavishly drenching you with the kind of compassion that a father offers his children—only infinitely better.

By praying, you're recognizing your status as a member of God's family. That means God the Father instructs you as you grow—yet another reason to worship Him.

Consider God's grace and pray the spiritual equivalent of a "yahoo!"—even if you find a better way to say it. Use prayer to offer personal praise.

While I'm amazed at what You can do, Father, I'm more amazed that You would want to help me. It's astounding to know that You want to be close to me. How could I keep from praising You?

LOVE LIBERALLY APPLIED

"God is spirit, and his worshipers must worship in the Spirit and in truth."
JOHN 4:24 NIV

God isn't like you—He's something altogether different. Your way of doing things isn't His way. He's a spirit, so no statue, picture, or idol could ever depict Him adequately, let alone garner your worship.

You've never seen the God you worship, so you accept Him by faith. You worship God, deferring to His methods and not your own. You worship God knowing that He is love and that He liberally applies His love to your life. You worship God because only in Him can truth be found.

When you worship, understand that God created you to thrive—not just exist. He gives good things (more on that tomorrow) that amplify His grace in your life.

Don't wait. Find a reason to praise God, seek His truth, and address Him in prayer. And then? Worship.

I worship You today, God, because You're different from me. You have wisdom I must learn and love I can experience—even when I don't understand it. I will pay attention to new ways I can worship You.

GIFTS

Whatever is good and perfect is a gift coming down to us from God our Father, who created all the lights in the heavens. He never changes or casts a shifting shadow.
JAMES 1:17 NLT

In the beginning, God created impressive gifts—good and perfect—and offered them to His creation. But it didn't take long for people to grow bored and dream up other amusements.

God is light, so He called His gift of light good. He then loaded the earth with other beautiful creations—all telling the story of an Artist who loves His creation.

God's greatest gift was His Son, who came down to us from heaven, walked among us, experienced what it was like to be one of us, and gave His life to pay the heavy price required for our rescue. The One who could've demanded your death because of your own imperfection chose to pay your debt instead. It's a gift you can't earn, and it comes with forgiveness, mercy, and eternal life.

The gifts kept coming—good and perfect gifts you can't afford but desperately need. Love brought grace. Hope encourages trust. Faith delivers peace.

There's nothing I have that You didn't give, Lord. You're good, and You bring gifts that are always worth more than I can imagine.

FORGIVEN AND LOVED FAMILY

God decided in advance to adopt us into his own family
by bringing us to himself through Jesus Christ. This is
what he wanted to do, and it gave him great pleasure.
EPHESIANS 1:5 NLT

Before you even needed to be forgiven, God wanted to forgive you. He chose to love you before your family did. God wanted you to be part of His family before you knew who He was. This pleased Him greatly, long before you accepted His forgiveness, love, and adoption.

You're very important to God. He thought of everything you would need to become a member of His family. In His mind, you were always adoptable—the only question was whether you would be wise enough to be adopted. Not everyone is, and that must make God extremely sad.

When the world needed love, God gave it. Everyone needs forgiveness, and God offers it. You needed a new family, so God invited you to join His.

When you pray, you're not just talking to a kind, benevolent God—you're speaking with your Father as His adopted son.

Help me get comfortable calling You Father.
You've accepted me into Your family, and I've
accepted Your offer. Let this journey continue.

HE KNOWS

*My frame was not hidden from you when I was made
in the secret place, when I was woven together in the
depths of the earth. Your eyes saw my unformed body;
all the days ordained for me were written in your book
before one of them came to be.*
Psalm 139:15–16 niv

Today's scripture is an Old Testament counterpart to yesterday's verse from Ephesians. God never says, "I did not see that coming." He can't be caught off guard. He observed your creation, but He knew you even before that. Before your body was fully developed, God had a plan for the life you would lead.

God knows all your decisions, good and bad. He has a book that records every day of your life—past, present, and future. Every event, meeting, and choice—He knows it all, so you can tell Him anything.

Have you ever wanted someone to love you despite the poor choices you've made? According to these verses, God doesn't love you because you are lovable. He just loves you—it's as simple and profound as that.

*I can't begin to understand why You love me,
God. All I needed to do was accept it. You already
knew me, and You still chose to love me.*

NO PERSONAL SPOTLIGHT REQUIRED

For by grace are ye saved through faith; and that not of yourselves: it is the gift of God: Not of works, lest any man should boast.
EPHESIANS 2:8–9 KJV

It would be incredibly disrespectful to believe that you've been saved by your own personal achievements and good works, not by what God has done. To boast of God's rescue as a gift you gave to yourself would be real audacity.

You might never say that, but have you ever felt that your good deeds need to outweigh the bad? God's grace has rescued you, and that's what your faith is rooted in. Grace is God's gift—not His work assignment.

If you think you need to balance the scales, you'll always be more intent on proving your own righteousness than praising God because He is righteous. When you pray, you might even start trying to list your accomplishments instead of thanking God for His.

Placing the focus on yourself makes it harder for you to see Him.

Help me to never get comfortable in thinking I can accept You as long as I do most of the work myself, Lord. Make me remember I could never do what Jesus did for me.

BOLD AND BLESSED

Let us come boldly to the throne of our gracious God. There we will receive his mercy, and we will find grace to help us when we need it most.
HEBREWS 4:16 NLT

Growing up, was it easy to ask adults for something? Often, they seemed to have no as their default answer. You might've wondered if anything could make them say yes. . .or if your questions were even worth asking. Sometimes, it was simpler just to stay quiet.

This attitude of frustration can also leak into your friendship with God. You may have a need but never ask. You might be unsure or fearful, so the words you're burning to say never leave your lips. You might not take your requests boldly to God—but that's exactly what today's verse asks you to do. In God's presence, at the foot of His throne, you'll find the mercy and grace that'll help meet your needs.

*I can be bold when I talk to You, Father.
Give me the courage to meet with You
knowing that You love and want to help me.*

COMPARISONS

Your righteousness is everlasting and your law is true.
PSALM 119:142 NIV

Life seems to teach you that people leave and that nothing is guaranteed, right? Even God tells you that humans are deceitful and selfish. But before you give up and wonder why you opened this book today, let's get to the good news: God is good, pure, and righteous—and He will never end. His law is truth—and it will never change. God never faces the struggles you face. Your questions about truth have never been mysteries to God.

When solving a problem, you might come to many conclusions, end with more questions than answers, and make decisions that derail your progress. But God has one conclusion, knows the answer before you ask the question, and makes perfect choices that keep your life on track.

When you pray, remember whom you are praying to. If you're searching for help, remember that God can do what you cannot.

Help me remember whom I'm talking to when I pray, God. I must remember that You have the answers I need.

TRUST

Quicken me, O LORD, for thy name's sake: for thy
righteousness' sake bring my soul out of trouble.
PSALM 143:11 KJV

You've probably been broken before, whether as a result
of others' decisions or because of your own. Your choices
can leave you prone to spiritual harm and forgetfulness.
That's why King David wanted God to rescue him—to bring
him back from the brink. He knew that God's righteous
faithfulness was the only rescue plan he could rely on.

When David needed an exit strategy, his heart tuned in
to the melody of God's grace—a song he wanted to sing.
This earthly king knew another King (God) whose name
would always be famous.

Don't halt your spiritual momentum by refusing to
trust in God to bring you out of trouble. Pray to Him when
you're in need, praising Him in advance for the help you
know He'll provide.

What resource could ever be superior to God? What
could prevent you from trusting Him? You may have a laun-
dry list of answers to that last question, but are they linked
to God or to your experiences with people? Failing to draw
this distinction makes trusting God much more difficult.

Rescue me, Lord. Help me
remember that's what You do.

BIG PLANS

*This is the plan: At the right time he will bring
everything together under the authority of
Christ—everything in heaven and on earth.*
Ephesians 1:10 nlt

Would you stay in a hotel that was built without planning?
Would you buy a car made from spare parts by a nonpro-
fessional? Would you feel comfortable touring the world
with a guide who's never traveled?

Plans are important—and the best plans are made by
those with the best knowledge of the subject matter. A
hotel's construction demands the plans of a skilled archi-
tect, a car needs a professional manufacturer, and any tour
requires a knowledgeable guide.

Every day, God confidently proclaims, "I have a plan."
Maybe you know this. . .but still keep going back to your
own plans or those made by friends and family. God's plan
doesn't drive His family apart—it brings them together.
That's unity.

So when you pray, ask God to reveal His plan and help
you follow it. Only the Great Rescuer's plan can make your
future incredible.

*I want to follow Your plan, Father. Give me
the courage to trust, the wisdom to follow,
and the desire to know You above all.*

ABOVE AND BEYOND

[God] wants all people to be saved and
to come to a knowledge of the truth.
1 TIMOTHY 2:4 NIV

Never think that God has plans only for a few people. He has one both for you and for your least favorite person. And it's the same plan. God wants people to know His truth—not just a few people and not just your friends. *All* people. No exceptions.

God knows that humans are a wayward lot. But even though they often refuse His offer, it still stands.

He plans for everyone to be rescued, so His resources never run short. He's willing to accept everyone, so His love overflows. He can forgive anyone, so He can forgive you. All you have to do is ask.

This is powerful, wonderful, exceptional news. It's the best offer anyone can receive. And it is God's plan.

Above my understanding and beyond my
expectations, You created a plan for everyone,
God. There's no limit to Your love.

THE ONLY ONE

"For this is how God loved the world: He gave his one and only Son, so that everyone who believes in him will not perish but have eternal life."
JOHN 3:16 NLT

There's another New Testament passage that complements the verse above. Romans 5:8 reminds us that "God showed his great love for us by sending Christ to die for us while we were still sinners" (NLT). God didn't wait until half of us stopped sinning—He sent rescue. People need forgiveness to obtain eternal life, so Jesus came to show how much God loves them.

Have you ever loved someone so much that you'd die in that person's place, even if that person deserved the punishment? In God's eyes, you were the convict. You broke His law, and you were condemned and ready to be sentenced. But then Jesus stepped into your world, taking the sentence your actions demanded. He died so that you can live, and He offers this love as a gift. He placed no condition on it, aside from the act of accepting the gift and believing that Jesus is the only One who could've done this.

What a profound truth, and what a reason to praise Him!

Lord, You give gifts to the man who has nothing and to the man who thinks he has everything. Your grace even applies to a man like me.

WHEN GOD LISTENS

If I regard iniquity in my heart, the Lord will not hear me.
PSALM 66:18 KJV

The word *iniquity* is another word for sin, which is the act of breaking one of God's commands. Even when you don't know you are breaking His laws, you're still sinning—and God never overlooks sin.

The verse above says that when sin is applied to your account, God becomes hard of hearing—a metaphor, of course, given that God can always hear you perfectly. But when you sin, you walk away from Him.

To better understand this illustration, picture a child who disobeys its parents. The parents are not obligated to grant that child's request. In fact, doing so would only reward the child's rebellion, leading to more bad behavior.

God never rewards disobedience, but He loves to forgive. So admit to God that you have broken His commands. Once your relationship is restored, God will listen and bless.

*Father, help me remember to confess
whenever I break Your law. May I return to
You and walk with You once more.*

NO DREAD

---

*[Adam] replied, "I heard you walking in the garden,
so I hid. I was afraid because I was naked."*
GENESIS 3:10 NLT

Staying outside of God's connection with you invariably leads to fear. When you break one of His laws and refuse to own up to your choices, God can seem like a fearsome judge, just waiting to condemn you. However, Romans 8:1 says, "There is no condemnation for those who belong to Christ Jesus" (NLT).

When Adam and Eve sinned, they suddenly saw their close friendship with God as yesterday's news. What was once their front-page headline was now impossible for them to believe.

Imagine the anxiety that people who do not walk with God must experience. To quell their fear of punishment, some simply choose to believe God doesn't exist. But God does exist, and merely thinking otherwise will not change this truth.

You don't have to run from God—just pray, admitting to Him your sin, and He will renew your relationship with Him.

*Feeling dread after I sin might drive me away from You,
God. Help me stay close so that I can remember You've
always loved me and don't want to condemn me.*

WORD WISE

*Before a word is on my tongue you,
LORD, know it completely.*
PSALM 139:4 NIV

You might read this verse and think, "Great, God knows every negative thing I will ever say." And you'd be right of course. But God also knows each small but significant step you'll take toward becoming a new creation. He knows all your future conversations with others about God's rescue plan. He knows when your words will demonstrate His kindness and love.

God even knows what you'll pray for—including all the requests that will reflect His heart. He's aware of each thing in your heart that will one day find its way to your mouth, as well as the ones that won't. You can't fool God.

Let this be a reminder that God knows both what you will say and what you should say. He understands your language, and He wants you to understand His.

*If I want to grow in my relationship with You,
Lord, I must carefully choose the words I speak
and pray. You knew I would say these words.
Keep changing them until they sound like You.*

A STUDENT'S PRAYER

*Let the words of my mouth, and the meditation
of my heart, be acceptable in thy sight,
O Lᴏʀᴅ, my strength, and my redeemer.*
Pꜱᴀʟᴍ 19:14 ᴋᴊᴠ

Think about yesterday's scripture, and then make today's a prayer. God knows everything you'll say, so ask Him to help you say the right thing.

By speaking this prayer, you're asking Him for the help you need. You want the God who created mouths to monitor what comes out of yours. You want God to be pleased with your thoughts.

The psalmist described God as the only One who could give him personal strength and reclaim his life from a destructive path. This is a prayer for restoration, transformation, and education. It is an admission that your old life was a failed experiment. It's a plea to be tutored by the divine Teacher.

*Father, may my prayers invite change—even if
it takes me to frightening, unexpected places.
It won't always be easy to let You alter my
mindset, but I believe it will be rewarding.*

CLASS IN SESSION

If you need wisdom, ask our generous God, and he will give it to you. He will not rebuke you for asking.
JAMES 1:5 NLT

You don't know it all. You may know lots of facts about a few topics, but let's face it—you're not an expert on everything. God is, though, and no amount of online tutorials can teach you what He knows.

Embrace this truth: you serve a generous God who wants to teach you what no five-step program ever could. He'll help you peer beyond chapter headings and memory verses, and as long as you keep asking, He'll never quit.

Class is always in session—what do you want to learn? What questions do you have from time to time? Don't feel awkward asking God for help. Today's verse clearly says He will give you wisdom, but first you need to ask. And if you refuse to ask, it might be time to tear down the wall of pride that lies between you and God's answer.

You're wise and I'm learning, God. Teach me. Give me answers. Thanks for not being upset when I ask. May I keep asking for Your wisdom every day of my life.

BETTER THAN CUSTOMER SERVICE

Wherein he hath abounded toward us in all wisdom and prudence.
EPHESIANS 1:8 KJV

Perhaps you've said the words, "I just had a gut reaction." This short sentence means you've either acted impulsively or applied an incomplete answer to a complex problem.

God never does that.

He has complete understanding, so He doesn't act impulsively. He doesn't have a deficiency in intelligence, so His answers are always complete. He gives a perfect response to each situation.

When you call a helpline, you expect to receive a comprehensive answer to your question. But God's helpline doesn't put you on hold. He never has to check with His technical department or spend time researching your question. He already knows what you'll say and what you need.

God doesn't respond to your crisis with a gut reaction, nor does He need to consult an online encyclopedia. God just needs you to have a willingness to talk with Him.

I don't need to listen to my gut when I'm listening to You, Lord. Thanks for tackling my tough days with Your generosity when I invite You into my life.

LOVE THOSE
YOU DON'T LIKE

---

*I am a friend to anyone who fears you—
anyone who obeys your commandments.*
PSALM 119:63 NLT

At one point, somebody has hurt you or someone you love. Whether intentional or accidental, the wound has perhaps festered into a constant reminder of the pain. Healing has been slow and marked with setbacks. But how much of your anguish is that person's fault? How much have you deepened the wound yourself by paying it too much attention?

If God hadn't chosen to show forgiveness, He might have destroyed everyone early in our history.

Many claim retribution as a right. However, without forgiveness, you'll feel wounds more deeply, trust people less, and have little reason to love as God has loved you.

God commands you to forgive. He gave you a heart to follow Him and love His people—and that love absolutely requires forgiveness.

I may not like everyone who follows You, Father, but You ask me to love them all. Stitch my heart to Yours, giving me Your compassion, kindness, and love. Help me walk with others as a friend because our journey leads to You.

ALL PEOPLE

*I urge, then, first of all, that petitions, prayers,
intercession and thanksgiving be made for all people.*
1 Timothy 2:1 niv

Praying for people makes it harder to desire bad things for
them. Could you really curse someone silently while asking
God to bless that person? If so, you'd be double-minded.
James 1:7–8 says such thinking results in personal instability
and an ineffective prayer life.

God wants you to thank Him for all people and plead on
their behalf. Doing so requires an authentic and transparent
prayer life that doesn't mask your true feelings.

By praying, you become a vital part of any community.
Others will need you to speak to God on their behalf. But
before you can sincerely pray this kind of prayer, you'll need
to start loving the people God loves—which is everyone.
You won't regret it.

*I need to pray sincerely for others, God—don't let
me get away with being deceitful. If sincerity means
sharing my struggles with You, then let me share.*

THE MASTERPIECE YOU OVERLOOK

You made all the delicate, inner parts of my body and knit me together in my mother's womb. Thank you for making me so wonderfully complex! Your workmanship is marvelous—how well I know it.
PSALM 139:13-14 NLT

Whether you accept it, deny it, or complain about it, God has made you "wonderfully complex"—and the same is true for everyone you meet.

God doesn't pay attention to only some people. As seen throughout the Bible, God works in the lives of believers and unbelievers alike. Jesus never sinned, but He wants sinners to come to Him. They are individual masterpieces, and He wants them to accept His rescue plan. He doesn't condone their actions, but He does whatever He can to make sure they know His love offers a way out of their self-imposed prison.

So when you pray for others, remember that no one lies outside the power of God's love.

The only difference between me and the worst sinner in the world is that I have You, Lord. You've accepted me, so help me accept others.

THE SHEPHERD OF SHEEP

Search me, O God, and know my heart; test me and know my anxious thoughts. Point out anything in me that offends you, and lead me along the path of everlasting life.
PSALM 139:23–24 NLT

Sheep aren't the smartest animals on the farm. They tend to wander away and fall into pits, and they can be easy pickings for predators. Because of their vulnerability, they require regular guidance.

Like it or not, the same is true for your relationship with God. On your own, you can't figure out what's really important in life—which is why you might find it hard to forgive, love, and help others sometimes. You will never realize the significance of such actions if all you see are the headaches they produce. Following the Shepherd (Jesus) won't seem appealing.

God knows your heart and tests your responses. He is fully acquainted with your anxiety. But when you sincerely seek His guidance, this same God will lead you into greener pastures.

Make me wise enough to seek You, Father. You know where I must go, so make me strong enough to follow.

THE MYSTERY

[God] made known to us the mystery of his will according to his good pleasure, which he purposed in Christ.
EPHESIANS 1:9 NIV

How can you learn anything if God isn't teaching? How can He teach if you don't listen? How can you listen if He doesn't speak? How can He speak if you won't pay attention?

As you might have noticed, these questions are trapped in a spin cycle: God won't teach if you're unwilling to learn. But you can break this cycle by becoming His disciple. Don't just shove His teachings into the back of your mind—listen to, apply, and share what you learn.

You might view discipleship as the act of moving to a quiet place, leaving everything behind to spend uninterrupted time learning about God. Some people might do that, but God has never required it. Being a disciple simply means following God, praying and intentionally searching His Word for answers to your mysteries.

And when you seek, God will help you find.

Following You is a treasure hunt, God. Help me seek Your truth so that I can know Your heart.

BE A CROSS CARRIER

*"If you do not carry your own cross and
follow me, you cannot be my disciple."*
Luke 14:27 NLT

You can be a Christian while not being a disciple, although such a decision is ill-advised. God's grace saves you and His love sustains you, but you can only become a disciple by consistently asking for His wisdom.

Discipleship comes at a cost that many aren't ready to pay. It involves taking multiple steps outside your comfort zone and maybe into persecution. You'll become highly visible, drawing anger and criticism from those who wish you'd shut your mouth and slip away from Jesus.

Often, carrying your own cross means something besides facing death. Discipleship rejects easy human interactions in favor of following Jesus. Jesus' disciples, for instance, left fishing, tax collecting, and a host of other jobs to make discipleship their prime objective.

As you learned yesterday, following Jesus may not require you to leave everything behind—but it will challenge you to consider your priorities.

*Help me take discipleship seriously, Lord.
Make staying in my comfort zone less
appealing than following Your lead.*

MORE THAN ENCOURAGEMENT

*Jesus said, "If you hold to my teaching,
you are really my disciples. Then you will know
the truth, and the truth will set you free."*
JOHN 8:31–32 NIV

The refusal to accept God's teachings often marks the beginning of bondage. Why? God offers truth, and rejecting that truth leaves you with only lies and half-truths. You then submit to bondage, always hesitant or confused about whether you're doing right.

Disciples, however, study the Bible and grasp its teachings with all their might. They pray to discover the truth, and the truth gives them the wisdom to know and the freedom to do what pleases God. No confusion—little hesitation.

A common misconception is that God just wants you to be happy. While He does want you to be satisfied—and happiness may spring from that—His goal for you is holiness, which enables you to trust every outcome to the work of God. This trust brings joy, which, unlike happiness, never depends on circumstances.

Disciples seek joy.

*Father, Your Son's words are more than a verse
of the day or even a source of encouragement—
they're life instructions that disciples follow.*

BE LIKE JESUS

*The disciple is not above his master: but every
one that is perfect shall be as his master.*
Luke 6:40 KJV

No matter how much Jesus teaches you, there are things
you simply cannot learn. As a result, you'll never be greater,
more important, or wiser than Jesus. You'll never know
everything He knows. But if you want to be more like Him,
become His disciple. Jesus never relinquishes His teaching
role, so you can become an expert in the things He says
are important.

Disciples share facts, not guesses, because they don't
just read about God's truth—they learn it. Discipleship will
lead you beyond this book (and the next). Discipleship
recognizes that if you want to be like Jesus and know
what He knows, you'll first need to learn what He teaches.
As a disciple, you'll want to digest God's Word and seek
His answers in prayer. The Bible says, "Taste and see that
the Lord is good: blessed is the man that trusteth in him"
(Psalm 34:8 KJV).

Chew on that for a while.

*You know my potential as a disciple, God. Help me start
following today and continue following tomorrow.*

THE THINGS HE SAID

Your eternal word, O LORD, stands firm in heaven.
PSALM 119:89 NLT

The Bible is no tabloid or gossip column. It's art, poetry, history, and hope. It's a letter from God that answers the questions of the soul. It applies to everyone, but not everyone will read it. It gives wisdom for the struggling, and like God Himself, it's changeless and holy.

Your prayers reflect your beliefs about the Bible. In his prayer, King David used the word eternal. He believed God's Word would last forever and that His thoughts are powerful and revered in heaven.

Believing only some of God's Word is problematic. When you doubt that God is the source of truth or believe that some of what He said doesn't work well today, you might start disregarding His other teachings too. As you read God's Word, you'll end up merely picking the things you already believe—or the things you want to.

Lord, help me believe that all Your words still apply to my life today. May I resist the urge to only accept what seems comfortable or familiar.

THREE STEPS

---

*"Ask and it will be given to you; seek and you will find;
knock and the door will be opened to you."*
MATTHEW 7:7 NIV

Scavenger hunts often require you to follow directions, ask
for help, and test possible doors to locate a "treasure." They
provide ample adventure and a reward for your search.

Prayer is part of the great scavenger hunt God has set
up for your life. It involves asking, seeking, and knocking—
but it's more than just a game. Asking is the prayer part of
your adventure. When you ask God for something you truly
need, He will provide it. In the seeking stage, you search
the Bible for answers to your questions. And knocking is
believing that God will open a door for you to explore. Perhaps this door will be an opportunity. . .or maybe a friend
to join you in your adventure.

*I don't often think of following You as an adventure,
Father. Help me step out of my comfort zone to
ask, seek, and knock. Thanks for Your answers.*

HELP WANTED

My help cometh from the Lord,
which made heaven and earth.
Psalm 121:2 KJV

Whether it's an unexpected check in the mail or the kindness of a stranger, any answer to your prayers is a gift from God—it's never just a coincidence.

The God who created heaven and earth cares about you. He pays attention to your needs, and He responds to them. Your prayers are an important part of that process, so share your heart, admit your needs, and ask for help. God sometimes says no to a request, but not because He's low on resources. He might say no because He knows what you really need, or maybe because pride has kept you from admitting God was right in giving you the rules you've been breaking.

Don't let anything block your communication with God.

On my own, I run low on resources and struggle
to make life work, God. Help me trust Your
ability to meet my needs, and keep my heart
tuned to Your plan, not to my own opinions.

GOD SPEAKS

"Don't be afraid, for I am with you. Don't be discouraged, for I am your God. I will strengthen you and help you. I will hold you up with my victorious right hand."
ISAIAH 41:10 NLT

Yesterday's reading encouraged you to pray when you need God's help. His help should be your first choice, not a last resort. Come to Him broken and desperate. Bring your anxiety and leave it with Him. Then read today's scripture one more time: "Don't be afraid, for I am with you. Don't be discouraged, for I am your God. I will strengthen you and help you. I will hold you up with my victorious right hand."

No fear—just companionship. No discouragement—He's your greatest resource. No desperation—He strengthens and helps.

Imagine your dad lifting you onto his shoulders when you were little, enabling you to peer over a crowd of adults. Or picture someone championing your personal struggles that were once marked with failure. That is what the Rescuer can do for you. Will you be rescued?

*Lord, You can take care of my problems,
so help me let You stop my worry.*

DRY, CRUSHED,
AND BECOMING CHEERFUL

A cheerful heart is good medicine,
but a crushed spirit dries up the bones.
PROVERBS 17:22 NIV

You've faced loss. It could've been anything you treasured—your job, a relationship, or even your health. And during these moments, as your life seemed to unravel, something shriveled inside you. What once flourished vibrantly as a byproduct of hope now seemed dry and ready to crumble. Are you feeling this way now? If so, don't worry: your situation is common.

God prescribes a cheerful heart as a remedy. But how can you be cheerful amid the pain of loss? Pray. Sharing your crushed spirit with the God who restores, repairs, and revives is the perfect place to begin. By refusing to pray, you accept loss as the final answer, feed your depression with morsels of despair, and lose stability in your spiritual spine.

When I pray, help me praise, Father. Remembering
Your goodness can shift my thoughts from
my current circumstance to Your always-
present faithfulness. May I watch You perform
a good work on my dry, crushed spirit.

COUNTERPRODUCTIVE

*Let your conversation be without covetousness; and be
content with such things as ye have: for he hath said,
I will never leave thee, nor forsake thee.*
HEBREWS 13:5 KJV

Have you ever caught yourself wanting to drive someone else's car, live where another person lives, or have the money someone else has?

The words jealousy, envy, and covetousness are similar but different. Jealousy is wishing that other people didn't have nice things. Envy is wanting what others have. Covetousness is taking what others have.

God wants you to be satisfied with what He's given you. His best gift to you is Himself—and He's not going anywhere.

Wanting other people's things—money, houses, and so on—is counterproductive when you already have God. Instead of being jealous, envious, and covetous, you'll start praying for others to have what you have. Nothing can compare to the God who never leaves or forsakes.

*You're God, and nothing anyone will ever
have is worth stepping away from You.
Keep me close as I walk with You.*

THINKING THROUGH

*Help me understand the meaning of your commandments,
and I will meditate on your wonderful deeds.*
PSALM 119:27 NLT

One of the goals of this book is to help you *meditate*—think through what the Bible says in a deeper way. Each entry only takes about three minutes to read. But afterward, you're always encouraged to spend as much time as you need thinking or meditating about what God may be trying to teach you.

Use today's scripture as a prayer to help you continue your journey, even after you close this book. You can even link this thought with yesterday's lesson about resisting the urge to want what others have. Once you're satisfied with the things you have, you'll have more time to think about the good things God has done and the ways He can do big things in your life. The more time you spend in envy, the less time you'll have to discover what God has already done for you.

*You have things to teach me, Lord. Help me
read Your Word with an engaged mind and
a willing spirit. I'm much better off following
You than chasing what's not mine.*

AFFLICTED

*Before I was afflicted I went astray,
but now I obey your word.*
PSALM 119:67 NIV

You have the ability to learn. Sometimes, your lessons are painful, and other times you learn from others' mistakes. In a best-case scenario, you accept God's truth and He helps you reduce your number of law-breaking incidents.

Today's verse indicates King David was afflicted—a word that means to be in pain, suffering, or trouble. Many things can cause affliction, but the king admitted that this happened because he went astray. David eventually returned to obedience, but not before his sin had carved a painful path through his life.

You may know what that's like—most people do. Sin can hurt you, your family, and your friends—and sometimes, even forgiveness and renewed obedience won't spare you from the consequences. When trust is destroyed and people are hurt, it often takes time to rebuild what was lost in a moment of sin.

*When I admit my sin through prayer, may I be reminded
of Your redemptive work, Father. Your mercy is
welcome as I relearn the value of following You.*

A MERCY GREATER

The LORD has told you what is good, and this is what he requires of you: to do what is right, to love mercy, and to walk humbly with your God.
MICAH 6:8 NLT

God has answered in His Word all your questions about goodness. What is good? Obedience to God's commands. What is the greatest command? To love. How should we love? With kindness, compassion, respect, righteousness, honor, humility, and mercy.

As this verse suggests, God wants you to love mercy. He gives this gift to everyone, so don't just embrace it for yourself—offer it to others too. Mercy is the act of withholding punishment from someone who is guilty. It's doing someone a favor, even when you don't owe one. It's an act of unexpected—but much needed—kindness.

God loves this kind of mercy because He offered it first. When you pray, ask God for a merciful disposition. . .and then share it with others.

God, I don't have to be the smartest in the room to know that You are. You want me to obey, offer mercy, and set my pride aside to walk with You. Let me do all three today.

THE WAYSTATION

*May your unfailing love come to me, L*ORD*,*
your salvation, according to your promise.
PSALM 119:41 NIV

Sometimes, bad days keep accumulating until you're at the breaking point. One more piece of bad news, it seems, will leave you undone. You feel like giving up, but even that won't solve your problems. You pray, but most words are left unsaid. And even if your eyes are dry, your anguish of soul is deep, wide, and treacherous. You feel like you're drowning with no help in sight.

This is an ugly place that no one ever brags about visiting, yet all men have been there. . .or soon will be. It's not a destination of choice, but a waystation for those waiting on a fresh supply of mercy.

You can't stay here, so you need someone to guide you out. Pray to God, allowing Him to rescue your heart from despair.

Lord, send an express delivery of Your promised
love and salvation. Right now, I can only survive
if You rescue me. I've always needed You, but I
recognize that I need You today more than ever.

TEAM BUILDING

[God] saved us, not because of the righteous things we had done, but because of his mercy. He washed away our sins, giving us a new birth and new life through the Holy Spirit.
TITUS 3:5 NLT

Maybe you remember being on the playground as a child. Two kids stepped up and declared they're picking teams, but they always picked the most impressive teammates first. Maybe they were the pickers' friends, or perhaps they were just good athletes. Regardless, everyone believed they got preferential treatment, and you sometimes got picked last. In retrospect, the whole process was unfair.

In contrast, our good deeds are not the reason God thinks highly of us. If they were, God would never notice anyone.

Your life can become new, but God has always been faultless. So when you pray, lock your mind on His perfection and thank Him for His grace. God doesn't choose His team based on ability, but on His mercy.

I can't do anything to improve my chances of being acceptable. You already chose me, Father, so there are no special skills required; I just need to be willing to be part of Your team—and Your team always wins.

DON'T STOP

Continue in prayer.
Colossians 4:2 KJV

God never suggested that prayer annoys Him. He did say, however, that you should never cease to have conversations with Him. Many things can merge with prayer—you've already read more than 130 examples, and there are more to come.

You could pray "It's me again, God" prayers, which often feel like you're reintroducing yourself to God after a long while of not speaking to Him. Or maybe they feel like you're asking Him to get you out of yet another mess.

But prayer was never intended only for emergencies. It's for daily use and emergency use. You talk to some people every day—maybe even ones you don't know very well. Your relationship with God is the best one you'll ever have, and it should continually inspire conversations.

Pray—and keep it going.

You never get tired of trying to talk to me, God.
Your Word shares Your thoughts, and You wait
for me to respond. You wait to hear my struggles,
my concerns, and my good news. Help me pray,
pray again, and continue to pray, because both
of us talk and listen in these conversations.

THE RESEARCH

*Worry weighs a person down; an encouraging
word cheers a person up.*
PROVERBS 12:25 NLT

Researchers once conducted a study to analyze how the six elements of prayer impacted people's well-being. The study group consisted of a few hundred participants, most of whom seemed to have a greater sense of well-being after praying prayers of adoration, thanksgiving, and reception. The opposite was true for confession, supplication, and obligatory prayer.

What's unclear is whether those participants follow God, have accepted His rescue plan, or read His Word. The researchers also stated that this was a subjective test meaning it was all based on the opinion of those being studied.

God supplies the truth, and you can either conform to it or turn your back on it. It's easy to understand why most would consider adoration, thanksgiving, and reception to be positive: these prayers don't involve things you personally want. Confession admits your sin, supplication admits you need help, and obligatory prayer (pray without ceasing) can make you feel that you have no choice. However, to the sincere heart, all forms of prayer bring relief.

*Lord, I shouldn't just pray to improve my well-being.
Prayer is meant to impact how I think about You.*

GOOD AND ACCEPTABLE

*For this is good and acceptable
in the sight of God our Saviour.*
1 TIMOTHY 2:3 KJV

You were created to worship God. You can do that through the words you say to others, the songs you sing, and the prayers you pray. God says that your prayers are good and acceptable from His point of view. This includes praying for friends, neighbors, and those who don't like you. Pray. It's "good and acceptable."

Yesterday, you read about a report on the kinds of prayer that enhance your well-being—but what if your prayer is meant to improve someone else's well-being? God may be ready to answer that person's greatest difficulty. So pray for everyone. It's good and acceptable.

It can be extremely hard to give God your anger, bitterness, and desire for revenge so that you can sincerely pray for others. But that too is good and acceptable.

Don't be afraid to ask for help. (Good and acceptable.) Confess your sin and admit God's way is right. (Good and acceptable.) Pray, even when you don't want to. (Good and acceptable.)

*You listen to my prayers, Father, and see them
as good and acceptable. Help me pursue
You, no matter what others think. Help me
love others, no matter what I think.*

STOP THE BABBLE

"When you pray, don't babble on and on as the Gentiles do. They think their prayers are answered merely by repeating their words again and again."
MATTHEW 6:7 NLT

God doesn't care about the number of words you say when you're talking to Him—He cares about your attitude and openness of heart. A string of memorized words doesn't capture God's attention. But your authenticity does.

You've probably borrowed phrases from others while praying. But when your heart and mind haven't connected to your words, you might be trespassing in the land of babble.

If people said the same thing every time they spoke to you, would you look forward to their visits? However, even when you struggle to vocalize the thoughts in your heart, God still welcomes you to talk to Him.

Think about your best conversations. Are they planned? Do you keep repeating yourself? Do you leave feeling satisfied with what you said? Try turning your prayer life into that kind of conversation.

Help me get comfortable praying, God. I don't want to be nervous when I talk to You.

MISPLACED CONFIDENCE

Trust in the LORD with all your heart and lean not on your own understanding; in all your ways submit to him, and he will make your paths straight.
PROVERBS 3:5–6 NIV

When you think you know best, you're treading on dangerous territory. It's one thing to be confident, but another altogether to know where your confidence comes from.

You've made mistakes, so stop leaning on what you think you know and start trusting in God's perfect knowledge. Since He knows everything, shouldn't you value His wisdom more than your own deductive reasoning?

Following God's directions may seem hard. You may not be able to see the benefit of quitting something you enjoy or beginning something you're not interested in. But obeying Him will lead you somewhere that makes sense and fulfills your purpose.

Once you're willing to submit to God's directions, ask Him for clarity and proclaim your desire to follow. Admit your faulty thinking and express your trust in His plan for you.

I've proven that I can't always trust myself, Lord. Help me trust You and then follow. Straighten my path and help me make progress.

WHEN GOD SAYS NO

Abraham approached [God] and said, "Will you sweep away both the righteous and the wicked? Suppose you find fifty righteous people living there in the city—will you still sweep it away and not spare it for their sakes?"
Genesis 18:23-24 NLT

Sodom and Gomorrah's unfaithfulness and disrespect toward God was generational, willful, and rampant. But when God told Abraham that He planned to destroy the cities, Abraham began to barter.

He started by asking God if He would withhold judgement if fifty righteous people could be found there. God agreed, and Abraham eventually whittled the number down to ten. God agreed once more. . .but the cities were still destroyed.

It wasn't that God refused to honor His promise—He just didn't find ten righteous people in Sodom and Gomorrah. He did find four, however, and He gave them time to leave before the destruction began.

This is the start of a few days' series on the times God says no. In this case, Abraham did not want to see these two cities destroyed, but God knew what Abraham did not.

Father, I may not understand when You say no. May I always remember that You hear my prayer. . . but that my prayer cannot stop Your plan.

CONSEQUENCES

"Sovereign LORD, you have begun to show to your servant your greatness and your strong hand. For what god is there in heaven or on earth who can do the deeds and mighty works you do? Let me go over and see the good land beyond the Jordan—that fine hill country and Lebanon."

DEUTERONOMY 3:24–25 NIV

Moses—sometimes called the deliverer—prayed these words. God had graciously said yes to many of his requests for food, water, and protection, and He had used Moses to perform miracles. God had even spoken with him on a mountaintop.

Moses followed God, served the people, and stood up for righteousness. He understood more than most how to have a conversation with God.

But he too had a moment of pride.

When Moses disobeyed God's order, God continued allowing him to lead—but He told Moses he couldn't enter the land God had promised the people.

Moses prayed to be allowed in, but God said no. Moses remained close to God, but he forfeited his opportunity to see the Lord answer his nation's prayer.

Even when You forgive me, God, sin still has consequences. May I always choose obedience to You over my temptations.

WISDOM DENIED

*Saul asked counsel of God, Shall I go down after the
Philistines? wilt thou deliver them into the hand
of Israel? But he answered him not that day.*
1 SAMUEL 14:37 KJV

Saul, Israel's first king, believed he was the most important
man alive. He was very good at disobeying God, so God
rejected him as king (see 1 Samuel 15:26).

Eventually, Saul became afraid and begged God for help.
But as today's verse shows, God didn't respond. Sin had
disconnected the king from the source of all knowledge,
reminding him of the importance of seeking God.

Saul needed wisdom, and God had already offered it.
The king just hadn't accepted.

When you reject the wisdom God offers, He might not
grant your request for more. Leave picking and choosing
for buffets, not for following God.

*Lord, I don't want to disobey and assume You'll
later give me wisdom that I'll like better. Help
me trust You enough to do what You say.*

DEPRESSION

---

*Then [Elijah] went on alone into the wilderness,
traveling all day. He sat down under a solitary broom
tree and prayed that he might die. "I have had enough,
LORD," he said. "Take my life, for I am no better than
my ancestors who have already died."*
1 KINGS 19:4 NLT

A mighty prophet helped prove that there was a God in
Israel, One who could choose when it would rain. The
demonstration was glorious, impressive, and definitive. Yet
when adversity came and the prophet felt threatened, he
told God he'd had enough. Now, he wanted to die.

But the God of all had other plans for Elijah. So when
God heard his prayer, He said no.

Elijah's prayer sprung from a place of depression, not
victory. He was living as a pessimist, refusing to recall the
glory God had just shown. It would not have been loving
or kind for God to have said yes to this prayer, given that
all this prophet needed was encouragement, rest, and a
little more time to see what God would do.

*Help me witness Your goodness, Father. Let me
remember Your victory. May I walk in Your presence.*

NO OBLIGATION

[The mother of James and John] said, "Grant that
one of these two sons of mine may sit at your right
and the other at your left in your kingdom."
MATTHEW 20:21 NIV

When the mother of two of Jesus' disciples asked Jesus if He could install her two sons just under Him as rulers, she was, at best, attempting to fulfill a personal favor; at worst, she was trying to instill obligation. Regardless, it was a bold request—and Jesus denied it.

The Bible isn't filled with examples of denied requests, but it does have a handful of them. God's Word proves that He can say no, but it also proves that He likes to say yes when it's in your best interest.

God knows where your request will lead you. If He knows it will give you a prideful mindset, why would He approve it? You'll never obligate Him to say yes to such a request.

You know my heart better than anyone, God.
Help me remember that You'll never agree to
any request that would lead me toward sin.

PERFORMANCE EVALUATION

"The Pharisee stood by himself and prayed this prayer: 'I thank you, God, that I am not like other people—cheaters, sinners, adulterers. I'm certainly not like that tax collector! I fast twice a week, and I give you a tenth of my income.'"
LUKE 18:11–12 NLT

The Lord's Prayer is a model that honors God and includes others, but today's scripture—found within one of Jesus' parables—shows us how *not* to pray.

The Pharisee favorably contrasted himself with all the city's sinners. His prayer served as a spiritual resume, presenting himself with a star pupil award. But this prayer directed no praise toward God, made no requests, and asked for no encouragement. It was a street performance.

Because the prayer made no request, God couldn't answer it. Instead, He treated it as unjustified. Nothing in this prayer invited God into human affairs. It possessed no humility, no repentance, and no joy.

This man didn't have God; he just had a solid personal performance. When you pray, don't use this tone. You're talking to a real God, so make real requests.

You're a good Lord, a caring Father, and a faithful God. May my prayers be a genuine expression of need and not a plea for a Better Than Most award.

A BETTER PRAYER

"The tax collector stood at a distance. He would not even look up to heaven, but beat his breast and said, 'God, have mercy on me, a sinner.'"
Luke 18:13 niv

This is the second half of yesterday's story. As a contrast to the bragging Pharisee, Jesus described a humble tax collector. Because tax collectors worked for the Roman government, taking money the people of Israel did not want to pay, they were generally hated, labeled as the worst of sinners and the most unabashed betrayers of their fellow citizens.

Maybe that's why the Pharisee tried to favorably compare himself to this man. Yet the tax collector had one humble request, and it had nothing to do with the Pharisee's insult: he simply wanted God to show mercy to him. The request was audacious, yet it touched God's heart. The man knew he needed grace, so God offered it.

What a fantastic prayer!

Father, You're not interested in a progress report; You want me to recognize that I need Your mercy to spare me from a lifetime of trouble. Please deliver mercy.

HELP

The LORD. . .is gracious to the humble.
PROVERBS 3:34 NLT

Humility in prayer means recognizing that God offers what you need and that you are not His equal. He will always be *more* than what you are.

You might be creative, but you can only create with the things God made first. You might write a beautiful song, but He created music. You might share a profound thought, but He gave you wisdom.

You can't show up in prayer as someone who has it all together. If you try, your prayers won't be genuine or authentic. God knows better.

You may think that God will be gracious to you if you share your progress. But God is nearest when you're crushed, humble, and broken-hearted. Why? Because that's when you cry to Him in total desperation, knowing He's the only One who can help.

You're ready to hear about my desperate situation anytime, God. I don't need to wait for an appointment. I have nowhere else to turn, and I want to turn to You. Hear me when I call.

BRING GLORY

---

*Wisdom's instruction is to fear the L*ORD*,*
and humility comes before honor.
PROVERBS 15:33 NIV

The Bible uses the word *glory* in a variety of ways, one being a term used to respect honorable people as important, powerful, or awesome. Applied to God, this respect is called "the fear of the Lord"—a phrase that reminds you to make God the most important part of any conversation, including prayer. Your personal humility offers glory to God. He takes note of the humble and gives them honor.

If prayer were a class, Professor Wisdom would tell you to give God glory, focus on His majesty, and allow your spirit to overflow with worship. These deeply personal prayers please God and ignite within you a desire for a closer walk, a deeper faith, and greater wisdom.

God knows who you are, and He wants to hear what you've learned about Him. Let what you've learned be the topic of your prayers.

I offer glory to You as my gift, Lord. I'm willing to share
what I have, even though You deserve more. Every
time I read Your Word, I'm amazed at how awesome
You are and reminded of how gracious You've been.

INFINITELY BETTER

Don't be selfish; don't try to impress others. Be humble,
thinking of others as better than yourselves.
PHILIPPIANS 2:3 NLT

Don't pray like you're in a ten-year class reunion. Trying to impress God with your accomplishments won't work—you could be spending your time on something infinitely better.

God already knows the things you've done and the attitude you had while doing them. Now He wants to hear about your next adventure. He wants you to invite Him to help you plan or adjust your schedule. He wants to know if you've been noticing the needs of others.

Don't try to impress Him or anyone else. Don't try to deceive yourself.

Thinking of others as better than yourself does not mean disregarding your own worth—it means elevating theirs. They are important to God, so their needs should be important to you.

When you're insulated inside a self-imposed bubble, it can be easy to assume that others have all the support they need. But do you? Probably not. . .and neither do they. Consider them important and invite them to walk with God alongside you.

I want to pay attention to what others say,
Father. Let them be so important to me
that I ask You about their needs.

THE YOKE

"Take my yoke upon you and learn from me, for I am gentle and humble in heart, and you will find rest for your souls."
MATTHEW 11:29 NIV

A yoke is a farm device that brings two animals together for a single job. The cooperation of the two makes it possible for more work to be done than if one of them tried to do it alone. A more seasoned animal works alongside a less-trained one, which is how the inexperienced creature learns.

Jesus compared that idea with your spiritual journey. As you walk forward with Him, He's experienced and you're in training. He's gentle and always does the bulk of the work. So take His yoke and walk with Him. You'll find rest because you'll no longer have to struggle alone.

His yoke does not restrict—it liberates you by helping you reach your destination. Jesus knows the way, and He will take the lead.

This life-changing connection is deeper than your best friendship. When you pray, remember this connection and consistently choose to follow His lead.

I want to walk with You, God. I want You to teach me where to step, how to help, and when to let You work. I'm grateful that You've let me take this journey with You.

THE UNTEACHABLE

Though the LORD is great, he cares for the humble,
but he keeps his distance from the proud.
PSALM 138:6 NLT

When you have no questions and believe there's little left to discover, you'll find it hard to learn anything new. You could read the Bible eight hours a day and still not learn much if you think you already know what you'll find.

We've talked a lot lately about the benefits of humility, but the core takeaway is that God helps those who ask for help and steps aside when pride suggests God shouldn't stand so close. You can access the best help you'll ever have, or you can go it alone. One sounds perfect. The other? Perfectly lonely.

It's no fun hanging around the guy who insists he's the smartest in the room, so imagine how God, who actually does know it all, feels when He tries to teach the unteachable. The proud are always the hardest to reach.

Lord, I don't want to be the guy who's certain
no one can teach him. I want to believe that I'll
learn something every time I encounter You.

THE WISDOM PRAYER

*Open my eyes that I may see
wonderful things in your law.*
PSALM 119:18 NIV

This is the prayer of the humble. It opens doors, invites instruction, and proclaims, "I don't know it all." It asks for God's companionship and declares that wonderful things can be found in the pages of His Word. . .and that you want to find them.

This prayer requests the corrective lens of God's law. It seeks clarity and answers. It indicates a thirst, a hunger, and a willingness to invest time.

Sincerely pray this prayer today—and never stop.

God wants to satisfy your curiosity, and He knows that the more you read His Word the more you'll learn. You can't know everything about a verse, chapter, or book in the Bible by only reading it once.

You're reading these devotions because you want to learn, be encouraged, and find inspiration to take steps in God's direction today. So incorporate your requests for wisdom into your standard prayer language.

*I need wisdom, Father. Give me insight. Help
me understand You, Your words, and Your plan
for my life. Teach me how to walk Your way.*

SWEET. SATISFYING.

How sweet are thy words unto my taste! yea,
sweeter than honey to my mouth!
PSALM 119:103 KJV

If you weren't learning anything, would you keep asking God to teach you? Digest this truth: God speaks through His Word. Praying for God to help you learn what He wants is not enough if you don't also read the Bible.

King David called God's words sweet and satisfying. They were filling and tasty to him, like food that he could access at any time and for any reason. Truth can be delivered to you like a favorite family recipe, and the more you eat, the more you'll want.

God's Word isn't a marketing message, but it is a message for everyone. It's not a book of poetry, but it can satisfy the poet's heart. It's not a novel, but it has great stories. It's not a history book, but it has plenty of historical lessons inside. Everything you need to know about God is found within the Bible. And remember: God wants to give you the wisdom to understand it.

I have no excuse for ignorance, God. I can ask for
wisdom and read Your Word, learning something new
every single time. Help me keep coming back for more.

THE BROADCAST

All Scripture is inspired by God and is useful to teach us what is true and to make us realize what is wrong in our lives. It corrects us when we are wrong and teaches us to do what is right.
2 TIMOTHY 3:16 NLT

How much scripture is inspired by God? All of it. How much scripture is useful for teaching you the truth? All of it. How much scripture can help you realize what's wrong in your life? *All of it.*

Don't open the Bible thinking you'll leave with a warm and fuzzy quote to share on social media. The Bible is a guidebook that's authored by the world's greatest Expert. It's the answer to your biggest questions.

Your prayers are transmitters that allow God to hear your life report at any moment—and God's Word invites you to turn on your receiver.

Broadcast your heart and wait. God will speak to you.

If life is a broadcast, help me share my life report with You, Lord. Thanks for writing Your reply long before I was aware I would need it.

WHY? WHY? WHY? HERE'S WHY.

"My Father's house has many rooms; if that were not so, would I have told you that I am going there to prepare a place for you?"
JOHN 14:2 NIV

Why pray if there is no God? Why obey if there is no reward? Why hope if there's no future?

Those who don't believe God exists see no need to follow His law. They can't express hope because they believe nothing is waiting for them beyond their last breath. They live in either fear or apathy. Their sense of purpose is minimized because they have nothing to look forward to, no higher power to learn from, and no reason to show compassion.

How pessimistic.

Thankfully, there's a better response. You can pray, expressing gratitude to God for giving you hope. You can be an optimist because God provides a purpose for your existence. You can obey knowing that God is preparing a place just for you.

You are a good Father with good plans and a great heart. You're real, and You've promised a future much better than my present. Thank You for offering a home and preparing it for me.

STRENGTH REQUEST

---

*My soul melteth for heaviness: strengthen
thou me according unto thy word.*
PSALM 119:28 KJV

Like a fallen autumn leaf under the first snow of winter
is a heavy-hearted man. He's filled with vulnerability and
weariness, sadness and deep sighing, depression and hope-
lessness.

King David knew that wallowing in self-pity was
pointless, so he prayed for strength. This is the kind of
circumstance-altering strength that comes from the Bible.

Think about this: David was a king. He had a powerful
army at his disposal. He was a fearless soldier. Yet he asked
for a strength he didn't have and couldn't buy.

His prayer should encourage you: you're not the only
one who's ever needed strength beyond your own. Or
maybe you've never asked for that strength, even when your
heart and mind remained heavy, oppressed, and numb. If
you haven't, are you ready to now?

*I need You, God. I need Your strength and Your hope.
I'm in life's deep end and I'm gripping the edge, waiting
for rescue. Give me strength and rescue me once more.*

US

May God be merciful and bless us.
May his face smile with favor on us.
PSALM 67:1 NLT

This Old Testament blessing resembles the Lord's Prayer, mostly due to the word *us*. There are other similarities (such as mercy and forgiveness), but the word *us* is such a powerful one because it connects the speaker with everyone else. It's inclusive. It doesn't pick and choose or leave people out.

The psalmist wanted God's mercy for everyone. He invited God's favor, and not just for himself. This is an idea worth revisiting.

If you haven't noticed, this book is trying to convince you that God wants to help you. He wants to hear your heart and meet your needs. But He also wants you to follow His example. Care for others because God cares for you. Accept His grace, and then show it to everyone. Ask for His mercy—for yourself and everybody else. Accept His favor, and then ask Him to show favor to others.

Don't ask God for something without wanting for others.

Remind me to care about others
and include them in my prayers, Lord.
May my prayers never be just about me.

BROKEN HEART

Streams of tears flow from my eyes,
for your law is not obeyed.
PSALM 119:136 NIV

David looked at his culture, listened to what people were saying, and wept. They were not following God. They were not reading His Word. They were not looking for His footprints.

The sight must've reminded him of a giant who had ridiculed, rejected, and refused to acknowledge God. David must have remembered defeating that giant—only to now see the giant's foolishness replaying in the lives of the people God had repeatedly rescued.

David didn't just have misty eyes or a lump in his throat. Tears streamed down his face, soaking his beard, blurring his eyes, and affecting his speech. His heart ached over his nation's sin.

When you see sinners who have impaired vision, hardened hearts, and unfocused souls, your prayers should express a broken heart for them. When you weep for the sinner, you weep for yourself. Pray that the things that break God's heart—in others and in yourself—start breaking yours as well.

The world would be a better place without sin,
Father. But sin exists in every human heart,
so I want all of us to follow You.

USE YOUR VOICE

May your ways be known throughout the earth,
your saving power among people everywhere.
PSALM 67:2 NLT

What faith it would take to pray this prayer! This is no "hide it under a bushel" request—you're asking God to make Himself known to every person on the planet. The answer to this prayer starts with you, so don't be shy. Make introductions.

God can make Himself known, of course, but what prevents you from sharing Him? Does it make you feel embarrassed, nervous, or awkward? If so, you're not the first.

Try this bonus prayer: "Make your ways known throughout the earth, Your saving power among people everywhere. And if You wish, give me the courage to be Your voice."

God can rescue lost and hurting people, yet it's easy for us to leave them lost and hurting when we misplace our courage. We have news that seems too good to be true—but it is true, and it's what these people need the most.

Help me make it clear that You're worthy, God.
Either remove my feelings of awkwardness or
give me the courage to ignore them. People
need to know You. Help me tell them.

PRAY FOR WORDS

*Be ready always to give an answer to every man
that asketh you a reason of the hope that
is in you with meekness and fear.*
1 PETER 3:15 KJV

When you pray, pray for words—words that help you understand what God is like, what He wants, and whom He loves. This prayer isn't just for you. As you learn more about God and understand more of what He wants, you'll want to share those words with other people.

To give an answer about God's hope, you must have the words. To be grateful for God's rescue, you need to know the Rescuer. To live in awe for God, you need to know why He inspires awe.

So use your words to pray for words, and read the Word so that you can share the words you learn. Once you do, you'll be able to give spiritual answers to those who wonder how those words have impacted you.

*I can call You Lord because I've accepted You. However,
I'll need to learn more about You to speak the truth
about You when others ask. Please enlighten me.*

THE ENTIRE NATION

May the nations praise you, O God.
Yes, may all the nations praise you.
PSALM 67:3 NLT

Asking God to move so mightily that entire nations stand up and honor Him is an enormous prayer. It often feels good to pray for people you know. You love them, so praying for them to know God seems natural.

But praying for an entire nation to praise God means praying for leaders, for people you think will never accept Him, and for people you need to forgive. These are exactly the ones you should be praying for. If you want your nation to honor God, you must set your hurt aside and give God room to rescue others. There are no loopholes.

God's love doesn't exclude anyone. It reaches out to all—and only those who choose to refuse His love can push Him away. This prayer breaks down walls, opens its arms, and welcomes God's best for everyone.

Father, may I care so much about others that I want everyone to accept Your rescue. I want to believe that You're big enough to rescue nations.

ON THEIR BEHALF

---

*[Pray] for kings and all those in authority, that we may
live peaceful and quiet lives in all godliness and holiness.*
1 TIMOTHY 2:2 NIV

The Bible tells us to pray for "those in authority." This includes mayors, governors, senators, congresspeople, the president, and law enforcement personnel.

Praying for them can be hard, especially when you don't agree with them. It's always been easier to tear leaders down than to raise them up in prayer—to wish they would fall than to pray they would govern well. It's a lot easier to stir the pot, causing anger to linger longer than it should.

Your prayer should begin with a hope—a destination in mind. What is this destination? A nation free from chaos and anger—or, as the Bible says, a "peaceful and quiet" place.

*Help me pray for my leaders, God. They have a big
job, and they need Your wisdom and strength to
lead with dignity and care. Even when I don't agree
with them, I do agree with You. So I will pray.*

GOVERNS AND GUIDES

*Let the whole world sing for joy, because you
govern the nations with justice and guide
the people of the whole world.*
PSALM 67:4 NLT

God's a great choir director who inspires a song within the hearts of His family. One begins to sing, and then another, and then the duet transforms into a choir and the choir explodes into a congregation as the song spreads and permeates hearts. It's a beautiful song that defines a joyful heart, invites nations to join, and declares God as the One who governs and guides.

Throughout history, God has occasionally been restored to national prominence. Such restoration is often called revival. You can't schedule or predict it, but you can pray for it and believe it to be possible. So whenever God breathes new life into a town, state, or nation, remember that He gets the credit. Just sing the song, declaring your joy over God's answer to the prayer you were brave enough to pray.

Ask Him to change the nation by first changing the hearts of its citizens. That would be a day worth celebrating.

*Change my world, Lord. Stir up stagnant
lives and revive complacent hearts. May I let
You work in ways that only You can.*

GOD VICTORIES

The king rejoices in your strength, Lord.
How great is his joy in the victories you give!
PSALM 21:1 NIV

By praying for your country and its leaders, you're believing in the power of potential. This kind of prayer affects eternal outcomes, but it also shapes current situations. It is powerful and relevant, unleashing God's sweeping plan in the form of revival.

Today's verse describes a leader who values God's power and finds joy in the victories only God could orchestrate. He recognizes that these victories don't result from his own plans—they are God's gift to a nation.

You don't possess this power, but you can ask God to use His power to make a change. Don't believe strategic planning alone can facilitate meaningful change—that's man's wisdom, not God's. God can frustrate your plans to help you understand that His plans are infinitely better.

Your plans are trustworthy, Father. Help me trust them.
They are wise. Help me understand. They are feats only
You can perform. Help me anticipate their success.

REPURPOSED PAIN

*I pray not that thou shouldest take them out of the world,
but that thou shouldest keep them from the evil.*
JOHN 17:15 KJV

You can learn from the trouble you face. Each struggle can either inject bitterness into your soul or guide you into God's refuge. You get to choose. Today's scripture shows how important your response is to God.

God does not tempt you. He never has and never will. But you live in a world populated with sinners, and their bad choices bring trouble—not just to themselves, but to you and everyone else. The Bible teaches that God can turn any bad circumstance into something good. If it causes you, or others, to trust in God or follow Him more faithfully, it has a good purpose.

Pray for God to repurpose your pain.

God, Your Son asked You to keep His disciples from evil. He wanted them to reject bitterness, revenge, and anger, leaving them free to follow Him on the tough days. This is exactly what You want for me whenever trouble threatens to destroy. Keep me from evil too.

ON TIME

*Listen to my cry for help, my King and my God,
for I pray to no one but you. Listen to my voice
in the morning, Lᴏʀᴅ. Each morning I bring my
requests to you and wait expectantly.*
Pꜱᴀʟᴍ 5:2–3 ɴʟᴛ

You'll never face life's greatest challenges alone, even when it feels that way. Believing that no one stands with you can make you depressed, but God stays by your side, ready to help. Cry out. Pray to Him. Then wait.

That last part is the hardest because when you pray, you want an immediate answer or response. Think of the times you've gone out to eat. You expect good service, timely responses, and attention to your needs. You might even praise the restaurant's service (with a tip) solely on account of the server's speed.

If this attitude bleeds into your prayer life, you'll start assuming that God needs to operate on your schedule and meet all your demands. He won't.

Pray, and then wait. When God says yes, He's always right on time.

*Thanks for meeting my needs, Lord. Help me
resist a demanding attitude. May I patiently
wait for You to show up and help.*

THE ASKING

Hear my cry, O God; listen to my prayer.
PSALM 61:1 NIV

Today's verse may sound like a condensed version of yesterday's, but it has another point to make.

Before God can listen to your prayer, you must recognize the issue, admit it's a problem, and then ask for help. When was the last time you did that? You might hate asking for help, refuse it when it's offered, and struggle solitarily for answers you'll never find alone.

It's possible to want God's help without asking. You might assume that since He knows everything, there's no reason to humble yourself and request His assistance.

Yes, God is aware of your dilemma, but if your pride prevents you from asking for help, He won't answer. God's not trying to make things hard for you—He just needs you to understand that your relationship with Him requires frequent conversations.

So start asking.

I might think I'm saving You time and trouble,
Father, but I often don't even understand
what I'm trying to accomplish. Give me the
strength to simply ask You for help.

GET ON THE PATH

*Guide my steps by your word,
so I will not be overcome by evil.*
PSALM 119:133 NLT

If God has taken the time to create a straight and narrow path that He asked you to stay on, why would you wander?

Imagine the narrow path, and then imagine a path as broad as a multilane interstate with multiple off-ramps and stops along the side. The first path takes you to your best destination (God), while the second leads you to destructive diversions. The second path is easier to travel, but each step leads you further away from wisdom.

In your prayers, ask God to supply the directions you need to walk with Him. Pray that you can resist the temptation to walk toward places of temporary enjoyment but long-term regret. Why waste time? Start walking the road you began when you accepted Jesus' rescue offer.

Your Word can redirect my steps, God, and this prayer can help me read the road signs. Lead me toward You and away from distractions.

CHANGE

Create in me a clean heart, O God;
and renew a right spirit within me.
PSALM 51:10 KJV

This is a prayer for men who don't want to hide anymore—
men who are tired of coverups and inauthenticity. This
prayer can remind you of the value of your relationship
with God. If your life is out of tune, pray to your Maker for
a factory reset.

This prayer recognizes God's ability to provide a clean
heart and a right spirit. It proclaims that God's intervention
is greater than self-help or positive thinking—even if both
are rooted in great intentions. Nothing compares to restoration from the God who creates and renews.

God offers a new life, not just a lightly repaired one.

Pray. Ask God to set your life in order, set your feet on
His path, and renew your spirit. This is a prayer God wants
to answer.

This is a hard prayer to pray, Lord. I want You to work
in my life in ways You've always wanted. Make me
clean. Make me brave enough to accept change.

LOVE OFFERED

Show us your unfailing love, O LORD,
and grant us your salvation.
PSALM 85:7 NLT

God's love is the most important asset you have. His love created you, holds you up, and invites you to His side. Accept the invitation—He won't change His mind.

The psalmist's petition was granted when God sent Jesus as the ultimate reminder of His love. That love is unfailing, and it offers salvation through God's great rescue plan.

Ask for a reminder of God's love—for you and those around you. They need His rescue too.

This is a prayer for moments of desperation, vulnerability, and uncertainty. Why pray only when you need help or only when you feel like worshipping God? Do both in the same prayer. Horrible days won't last forever, but neither will perfect days. Take everything to God—His love is your welcome mat.

I'm overwhelmed by Your goodness, Father. That
goodness has partnered with Your faithfulness
and love to rescue me. Show this good news
to others who need it as much as I did.

THERE IS NO SEARCH ENGINE

---

*"Call to me and I will answer you and tell you great
and unsearchable things you do not know."*
JEREMIAH 33:3 NIV

Sometimes, God's teachings can seem mysterious and hard to understand because they're very different from your usual experiences. But they aren't mysteries to God. They're just the right way of doing things.

Whenever you pray to a God whose ways are different from yours, His answer probably won't match your expectations. And if that doesn't seem acceptable, remember that He instructs in "great and unsearchable" ways. You can't know or understand these things on your own.

These answers aren't found in a search engine, encyclopedia, or dictionary. Even the answers in this book are no substitute for your conversations with God. His words will apply directly to your circumstances, forming an overwhelming, intensely personal connection between you and Him.

*You're the God of better answers and
personalized promises, and You're the source
of all strength. I have questions and You have
answers. Help me understand Your teaching.*

THE NEED OF EPAPHRODITUS

---

*My God shall supply all your need according
to his riches in glory by Christ Jesus.*
PHILIPPIANS 4:19 KJV

God views love as the act of sharing what you have with those who need it, reducing your own resources to add to theirs.

The Lord used a man named Epaphroditus to meet the needs of the apostle Paul. After receiving help from his friend, Paul proclaimed, "God shall supply all your need according to his riches in glory by Christ Jesus."

The apostle put himself on top of the "Most Sinful" list. He had persecuted Christians, but when he chose to follow Jesus—the very One he had sought to destroy—he was promised a new life and everything he needed to live it. That's why he was certain God would care for you too.

As Paul assured Epaphroditus, God won't overlook your kindness. So give, share what you have, and walk with the lonely. God knows what you need. He'll never ignore you or show up late.

*Help me remember that You'll never stop
being good, Lord. Help me show others
that You can take care of them too.*

GESTURE OF GRATITUDE

*Let us offer the sacrifice of praise to God continually,
that is, the fruit of our lips giving thanks to his name.*
HEBREWS 13:15 KJV

Over the past six months, we've only grazed the surface of
how powerful a man's prayers can be. These prayers are the
best line of communication between your heart and God's.
His answers should cause worship to bubble up from the
core of your being and into God's ears. They should deliver
awe, inspiring you to glorify Him.

If praise is a sacrifice, it pales in comparison to the gifts
that inspire it. Show gratitude for God's all-encompassing
rescue plan, for His love that inspires forgiveness, and for
the people God has sent into your life so that you can pray
for them.

Worship the God who answers prayers, instructs you
when you need wisdom, and rescues you when no one else
can. Worship. . .then worship again. Remember God's goodness, and then start counting His blessings all over again.

*Father, many people have helped me grow in my
work, faith, and life, but no one can ever help
me as much as You do every day. Whether I'm
lying in bed, driving, or seeking encouragement,
You listen, reassure, and teach. I'm grateful.*

RICH

---

*I rejoice in your word like one who
discovers a great treasure.*
PSALM 119:162 NLT

You don't need an impressive portfolio, 401k, or bank account—if you follow Jesus, you're rich. You could deny it, and most people would agree with you. . .if you both believe that riches are defined by money.

God's riches have been yours from the very moment you accepted His rescue. Here's a short list: He made you His child, He spared no expense in equipping you for this new life, He's promised to meet your needs, and He's preparing you a home with Him that you'll enter once this one's over. This list doesn't even include the treasures you'll find in His Word. Everything you need to know about living like Jesus is found in those pages.

Thank God. He's lavished His love onto you. Praise Him for seeing you as valuable enough to give what meant the most to Him so that He could reach you.

*I find it hard to believe You could love someone
like me, God, but the evidence is in: You do,
and You always have. As long as I recognize
this truth, I'll never run short on treasures.*

A FIGHT INITIATED

The Lord is faithful, and he will strengthen
you and protect you from the evil one.
2 THESSALONIANS 3:3 NIV

To protect you against the evil one, God has given you armor that you can't manufacture on your own. Your greatest command as a soldier is, "Stand firm." Don't initiate your fight with the adversary, but don't run either. Just take your stand.

When you decided to follow Jesus, Satan was so upset with your decision that he now sees you as an enemy to kill. If Satan can't claim you, he wants God to see you destroyed.

Stand fast, gain strength, and discover God's protection. The undeserved benefits of your new life stretch beyond expectations, and you can share them freely with all. So start sharing.

Prayer isn't a duty—it's an opportunity and a privilege. It allows you to talk to God about anything. It's your strongest connection to the faithful God who's never abandoned you. That's just as true now as it was before you were born, and it will be true long after you take your last breath.

As for today? Stand.

I want to stand, Lord. I need to. Thanks
for giving me the tools to learn how to be
faithful. Thanks for being faithful first.

THE HOPE INCREASE

*Rejoicing in hope; patient in tribulation;
continuing instant in prayer.*
ROMANS 12:12 KJV

Prayer is a celebration of conversation. It's an exchange of ideas that teaches and provides companionship wherever you are. It's a potent part of life for the follower of Jesus Christ.

Today's verse summarizes the core truths you've read so far:

- Hope is a rock-solid trust in a never-changing God. Rejoice.

- Everyone struggles, so be patient when you pray. Help is on the way.

- Prayer includes God in your daily conversations.

Hope is trust, not wishful thinking; therefore, your faith in God's great outcome can help you endure hard times. When you are certain God will show up, you'll pray more throughout each day.

Ask for courage, spend time thanking God for taking care of you, and pray for others. Inject hope, patience, and praise into your prayers, always discovering more things to pray about.

The more I pray, the more I feel comfortable calling You Father. Let me find joy in hope, patience in struggle, and purpose in my prayers. Help me know You more.

PRAYING HIS PLAN

Because we are united with Christ, we have received an inheritance from God, for he chose us in advance, and he makes everything work out according to his plan.

Ephesians 1:11 NLT

When you pray, it can be easy to think you're the only one. But you're not. Whether they're driving to work, at the gym, or in a cubicle, people everywhere are talking to God and asking for His will to be done. They want to see the best for others. They don't have the answers, but they know God does.

That's the team you're on today—millions of people who are following Jesus through confusing circumstances. So stand united with your fellow Christians in asking God to do the impossible.

Read today's verse again: God makes everything work out according to His plan. He doesn't need to ask you how you think things should go; as He's repeatedly proven, He can turn the worst circumstance into something incredibly beautiful. Expect God to keep surprising you, and join with others in praying for His best.

I pray with others, God, so may our conversations please You and eagerly seek Your answers to our problems.

KEEP PRAYING.
KEEP LISTENING.

"My sheep listen to my voice;
I know them, and they follow me."
JOHN 10:27 NIV

God knows your voice. There is never any confusion when you call. You don't even need to mention your name—He knows you.

However, prayer can introduce God's voice to you. It may not be audible, but it's highly recognizable. As you read the Bible, God often speaks directly to your need.

He knows you and loves you, so listen to His voice. Follow His lead.

Consider everything you've read and the prayers you've prayed. Think of ways you can convert what you've learned into personal prayer.

This isn't the end of a book—it's the start of an adventure. The journey wasn't a six-month pep talk—it was a call for you to make prayer your new normal.

Don't quit after you close this book. Keep praying.

You don't want me to think of prayer as obligatory,
Lord. You want me to relish the opportunities to pray
in this moment, five minutes from now, and every
day of my life. Thank You for never getting tired of
hearing from me. Remind me to come back soon.

ABOUT THE AUTHOR

Glenn A. Hascall is an accomplished writer with credits in more than 140 books, including multiple titles in the Brave Boys, 3-Minute Prayers, and 3-Minute Devotions series. He has provided ghostwriting services on several additional books, and is also a broadcast veteran and voice actor actively involved in audio drama.

A husband, dad, and grandfather, Glenn is a former mayor with a city park named after him. And he is an Admiral in the Great Navy of Nebraska, a honorary (and ironic) title bestowed by a former governor.

ANOTHER GREAT DEVOTIONAL FOR MEN!

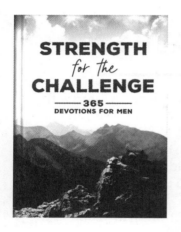

Guys, you know life can be tough. But never forget that God is strong. This daily devotional builds off the inspired truth of 2 Corinthians 12:10, "when I am weak, then I am strong." You'll be encouraged to seek your daily strength from the all-powerful God through Jesus Christ.

Hardback / 978-1-64352-850-2 / $16.99